SWILL 2015

Neil Williams

Vile Fen Press

a division of Klatha Entertainment an Uldune Media company

SWILL 2015
Copyright © 2025 Neil Williams

Library and Archives Canada Cataloguing in Publication

Williams, Neil, 1958-
(Jamieson-Williams, Neil, 1958-)

SWILL 2015 / Neil Williams.

ISBN 978-1-894602-34-1
    1. Science fiction--History and criticism.

2. Science fiction fans. I. Title.

PN3433.5.J36 2012   809.3'8762   C2012-901693-4

Published by Vile Fen Press
an imprint of Uldune Media
504 – 635 Canterbury Street,
Woodstock, ON, Canada, L4S 8X9.
www.uldunemedia.ca

Table of Contents

Introducing SWILL 2015

And here is where the shift begins. It is here that
the move away from being a quarterly zine, with a
special annual issue, to that of having two issues per
year and a special annual issue, does begin.
Eventually, there would just being an annual issue.

This made sense at the time as it was very clear that
there would be no research project on science fiction
fandom. I would either not be permitted to use my
academic affiliation to obtain funding for the project
and, if I financed a smaller project myself, I would
not be permitted to publish academically using my
institutional affiliation. Thus, one of the major
reasons for reviving SWILL (other than the thirtieth
anniversary) had gone.

Thus, the main reason for publishing SWILL was now,
just because. And the decision to move in the
direction of publishing annually made sense.

In this volume, both of the annual issues are devoted
to Puppygate and the Hugos. I have never been a great
supporter of the Hugo Awards and I continue to view
them as the Peoples' Choice Awards of speculative
fiction, and view the Nebula Awards as more valid.
Nevertheless, the hijacking of the Hugo Awards system
by voting slates and the right-wing of fandom did not
appeal to me. Both issue #28 and issue #29 are not
devoted to the Puppygate debacle.

Enjoy...
Neil Williams
August 2024

TRIGGER WARNING

SWILL is written to BE OFFENSIVE. Really, this is one
of the premeditated intents of SWILL. It was written
to offend back forty years ago and also in more recent
and contemporary years.

It was not written for the sensibilities of those
people under 30 years of age in the mid 2020s.

If you are the type of person who becomes so very much
traumatised, that you have to curl up into a ball in
bed for a week, after watching an episode of Friends
where Chandler Bing talks about his father. If you
thus find the 1990s sitcom Friends too racist, sexist,
homophobic, and transphobic to watch, and you believe
in the core of your heart, that this television series
should never, ever, be permitted to air again and that
all of the recordings and mastertapes of the series
MUST be destroyed so there is now no danger that you
will ever encounter this television show ever in the
future; then SWILL is definitely not for you.

SWILL is offensive to many. That is one of the main
purposes of SWILL. Read at your own risk.

You have been warned.

SWILL

#27   Annual 2015

Table of Contents

SWILL is published quarterly (Spring, Summer, Autumn, and Winter) along with an annual every February - in other words, five times per year.

SWILL

Issue #27 Annual - June 2015

Copyright © 1981 - 2015 VileFen Press

a division of Klatha Entertainment an Uldune Media company

swill.uldunemedia.ca

Editorial: A Perfect Shit-Storm

Neil Jamieson-Williams

This issue is very late -- this is a hobby, people, not an occupation, and the demands of ordinary life and work can get in the way[1] -- and there has been a whole shit-storm that has exploded in my "absence". So let's get to it...

Fandom has changed. SWILL has devoted many, many words on this topic and I will, somewhat breifly, summarise my analysis of those changes as they lie at the foundation of the issue at hand -- the Puppies. Fandom today is very diverse; it is no longer a single, small, unified (as there was really only one dominant medium -- print), literary genre[2] subculture, but an umbrella term, for a large supragenre (SF, Fantasy, Horror, and other speculative fiction), within which there are a multitude of subgenres and subsubgenres and content mediums. It is not longer (as the Puppies harp on about) the 1970s -- nor is it the 1990s for that matter. Growth has its benefits -- you are no longer a weirdo because you like SF & F, because almost everybody today likes SF & F to some degree (otherwise there would not be the ammount of speculative fiction, or weakly linked speculative fiction, programming that exists on television). But growth does create new problems and one of those problems is unity.

Unity in fandom??? What is this idiot talking about? Doesn't this punk know anything about fan history? Blah, blah, blah! Yeah, I do know something about fan history (I'm an old punk) and the stupid feuds, and snail-mail flamewars of days gone by, etc. I'm not saying that fandom was ever unified, but in the past it was somewhat more unified, because the genre was more unified. Certainly, even in the eighties, there were the born-again Trekkies who would watch and read only Trek and Trek-related content and the D & D gamers who would behave in a similar fashion, and yet, there remained more of a general unity within the genre. SF & F was like a small town, with some monster homes being built on the edge of town and inhabitted by people who,

---

[1] Yes, Taral; I do realise that this is further evidence of my unfannishness. Please feel free to revoke my traditional fan status...

[2] Sorry, well not really, Puppy-dogs; however the fact remains that science fiction and fantasy (as well as horror and weird) all began as genres within literature (the print medium). The hated term "literary" pertains to all literature and to the genre of literary realistic fiction.

although they would shop in town, didn't really fit in. They
didn't know the history, the local politics, the norms and values
of the town -- they were outsiders who shared one thing in common
with the established residents; they really liked living in the
town. The Speculative Fiction supragenre is similar to that
small town being absorbed into a nearby city -- the overall unity
and identity has either been lost or severely erroded. Yes, we
all love, or at least like, Speculative Fiction but this is a
weak unity and a weak identity -- just, an umbrella identity that
doesn't really say very much about anything. And so, the
subgenres that existed with SF & F have proliferated and bred
subsubgenres and fandom has fragmented[3] into a myriad of fandoms
and subfandoms and certain terms have either lost their meaning
entirely or mean different things to different fans.

Speculative fiction, what do we mean by the term? It means that
the setting takes place within a speculative world (imaginary
country, the future, an alternate timeline, etc.) or within a
realistic setting wherein a speculative element or group of
elements are operating (a fantasy realm inteacts with our mundane
world, vampires actually exist, a spaceborne plague infects
humankind, etc.). In other words, it is not realistic fiction.
Beyond that, there is a lot of variety -- a fucking humungous lot
of variety. That means that the audience that enjoys the
subgenre of military SF is not necessarily the same audience that
is going to enjoy the subgenre of YA supernatural romance -- in
all probability, these two audience segments mean two very
different things when they say that they love speculative
fiction. There is nothing wrong with this situation or with the
"big tent" that speculative fiction has become; it does mean that
within that supragenre, there is no longer a strong unifying
bond, nor is there one within the established genres, e.g. SF,
nor does it exist within the established subgenres, such as
Alternate History.

As goes the genre so goes fandom -- which is composed of those
people who are fans of the genre. The emergence of the
speculative fiction supragenre has created the suprafandom, on
one hand, and microfandom -- or subsubfandoms (like those who are
only fans of a particular television programme or game, and its
related media) -- on the other hand. Fandom today is also a
"big tent" and therefore the meaning of the term "fan" has become

---

[3] I prefer fragmented to the term balkanised. Balkanised implies that there
is an intent to wall yourself off, to seperate yourself, from other subfandoms
rather than simply choosing to consume a different subgenre/subsubgenre.

more inclusive and has been debated, often with grinding axes and intense flamewars. The most inclusive definition of a fan is someone who is a content consumer of speculative fiction who also engages in some form of fan activity (this also has a wide range of forms and types) -- if you do not participate or engage in any fan activity, you are just a genre consumer, not a fan. That said, the type of fanac that you engage in, does determine what type of fan you are and there are two major typologies present today (with a lot of cross-over nodes and microfandom activity that straddles the boundaries and other fuzzy bits) that form a dichotomy within present day fandom.

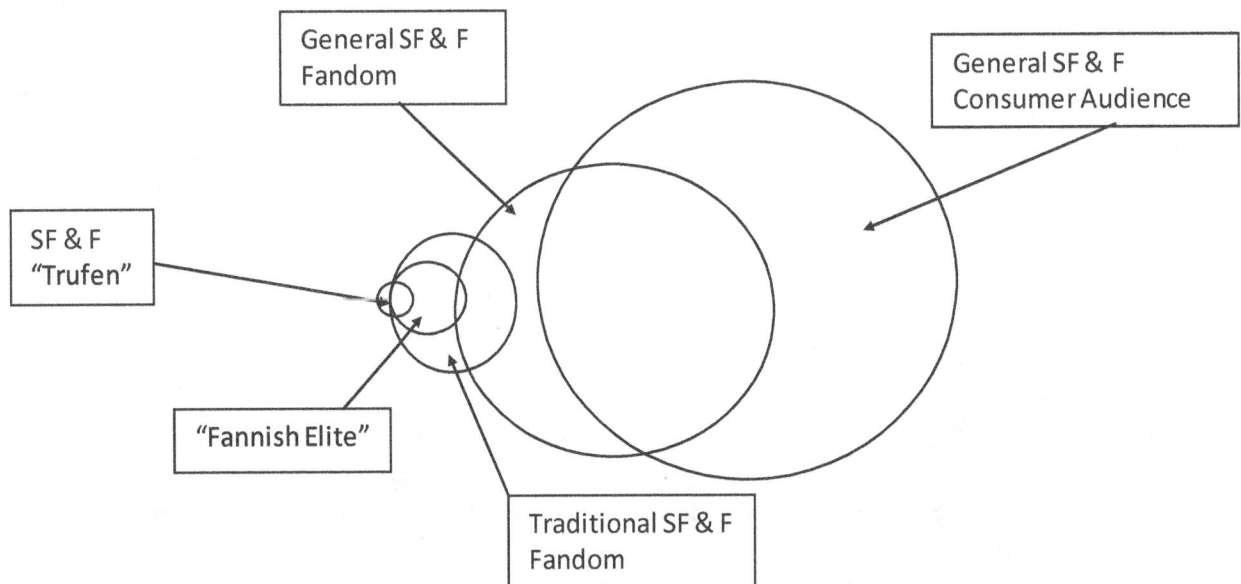

The two major dichotomies refer to fandom, only. The general SF & F consumer audience largest is the consumer of speculative fiction content; this audience is often oblivious that fandom even exists or are uninterested in fandom. period. Within fandom, there is general SF & F fandom and traditional SF & F fandom. These are two very different fandoms. The general fans tend to be digital natives or have adopted digital native fanac as their dominant or sole form of fan activity. The general fan places more emphasis upon specific subgenres that they enjoy, primarily uses social media for fanac, they have little knowledge of fan history, they see other media as primary over the print medium, and they attend trade show conventions (e.g. FanExpo,

ComicCon) over fan-run conventions. Just as the general SF & F consumer audience vastly outnumbers general fandom, general fandom vastly outnumbers traditional fandom.

Traditional fandom tend to be digital immigrants or have adopted (within fandom) digital immigrant modes of fan activity. The traditional fan places more of an emphasis upon whole genres or large segments of subgenres within specific genres (though some may place primary emphasis on a specific franchise, e.g. Star Trek or Star Wars[4]), although they probably use social media they use it differently or sparingly or as a means to co-ordinate face-to-face fanac, fanac includes publishing fanzines and conrunning, they have some knowledge of fan history, they tend to see the medium of print as the primary medium (though they also consume within other mediums), and they attend fan-run conventions over trade show conventions. Traditional fandom can also be exclusive and many view general fans as no different than the consumer audience -- i.e. they see general fans as being mundanes. Within traditional fandom there is a subsegment that calls itself "trufen" (true fandom) and this segment subscribes to the predominant norms and values that existed in SF fandom prior to 1995 (and in some cases prior to 1980); hardline "trufen" regard the rest of fandom as being one and the same as the consumer audience -- everyone who is not a "trufen" is a mundane.

The so-called Worldcon Fannish Elite, that the Puppies are in rebellion against, is composed of those people who regularly nominate and vote for the Hugo Awards. These are also the people who bid, vote on bids, and participate in running the Worldcon. These also tend to be people who are part of traditional fandom over general fandom. Why? The most probable and logical reason for this is that conrunning (of fan-run conventions) is a form of fanac done by traditional fans and not by general fans; the Worldcon is a fan-run convention and the Hugo Awards are organised by the Worldcon. The claim by the Puppies that a cabal of literary, leftist, feminist, academic, LGBT, "social justice warriors" are operating the Hugo Awards like a secret society in

---

[4] Because these are pre-digital franchises, the norms and values within the fandoms for these franchises are more alligned toward that of traditional fandom.

opposition to the tastes of all general fans is nothing more than that, a claim -- and a bullshit claim at that. Yes, the Worldcon has not proactively reached out to general fandom (which is not surprising as many of the movers and shakers in conrunning view the average general fan as being a mundane -- a non-fan). But, this is no eevil conspiracy. And because traditional fandom tends to have some connexions to the publishing industry and values the publishing industry over the content producers of other mediums, there is a strong print bias.

While some of the Sad Puppies criticisms of "the way things are" do have validity and should be listened to and discussed, their final analysis and their claim that they are representative of general fandom is absolute fucking chickenshit. Neither of the Puppies are any more representatve than the supposedly evil Worldcon fannish elite -- they are also a small and unrepresentaive segment of the SF & F fan population.

Both the Sad Puppies and Rabid Puppies are the fannish equivilant of urban guerillas or terrorists. They have both voiced the intent to "destroy science fiction" and to "destroy the Hugos". The hijacking of the 2015 Hugo Award nominations by the Puppies is nothing more than a terrorist attack against all of fandom by groups who claim to represent all of fandom, but only represent a tiny minority, possibly a smaller minority than the Worldcon fannish elite they are supposedly attempting to "save" fandom from.

Speculative fiction (including SF) has grown, become successful, and accepted (not within the literary fiction establishment -- a definite cabal -- that is probably less representative of the reading population than the Puppies are to speculative fiction) in global culture as an ordinary and normative genre (just like medical dramas, police proceedurals, etc.). There are consequences to growth and acceptance; the Puppy terrorists are, unfortunately, one of the negative consequences.

Thrashing Trufen: The Hugo Awards...

Neil Jamieson-Williams

There is a major controversy in fandom regarding the Hugo Awards and the legal (in letter, though not in spirit) hijacking of the nomination process by a group of Christian falangist fans. I am not going to discuss the merits, or lack thereof, of the Sad and Rabid Puppies (at least not here -- see this issue's Flogging a Dead Trekkie). Instead, I will attack the Hugo Awards as an institution and as the hallmark of the best in SF & F.

First, the claim that this is the premier award in SF & F... It is definitely the oldest award in the genres, and that made it important, when it was the only award. But, it isn't the only award. Like it or not, the Hugo Awards are SF & F's version of the People's Choice Awards -- voted on by the general public. Therefore, it does not have the same prestige or credibility as the Nebula Awards which, like the Academy Awards, are voted on by a professional association of content creators (which doesn't mean that there are not flaws in either the nomination or the voting process of the Academy Awards or the Nebula Awards, just that these awards are peer-judged rather than audience-judged).

Second, the Hugo Awards (though this has been improved somewhat over the past 30 years), even though they are supposed to be an international award, still remain, mostly an American award. The Nebula Awards (though the award of an American professional association) tend to have a more international focus than the Hugos do. The USA focus of the Hugo Awards is why there are now all the various national awards; Auroras and Sunburst (Canada), BSFA (UK), Grand Prix de l'Imaginaire and Prix Rosny-Aîné (France), Aurealis Award and Ditmar (Australia), Deutscher Science Fiction Preis (Germany), Aelita Prize (Russia), to name a few.

Three, although the nomination and voting process is open to the general public -- most of the SF & F audience is unaware of how the process works and how they can participate. Thus, the nomination and voting is skewed toward active science fiction and fantasy fans as opposed to the general audience for the genres.

The vast audience of genre readers and viewers do not know that one just has to purchase a supporting membership to the Worldcon to engage in nominating and voting for the Hugos -- of course, the majority of that audience is also unaware of the existence of Worldcon, as well. Thus, the Hugo Awards are not really representative of the SF & F audience as a whole (a Some-of-the-People's Choice Award).

As there are usually between 800 and 1,500 ballots cast (sometimes as high as 2,000) and because usually only active fans (as well as writers and editors) participate in the nomination and voting for the awards, the entire process is open to the controversy that now embroils the Hugos -- slate voting and block voting. This has happened before when L. Ron Hubbard's *Mission Earth: Black Genesis* was nominated as best novel in 1987 due to massive Church of Scientology block voting - it didn't win. With the audience fragmented into subgenres, it was only a matter of time before slate voting emerged to benefit one subgenre over another.

That said, the appearance of an authoritarian, right-wing, Christian falange slate was a surprise to me (and probably others as well)...

Pissing on a Pile of Old Amazings:

...a modest column by Lester Rainsford

Lester has often wondered why, analagously to 'catapult', there
is no such thing as a 'dogapult', which would hurl the yipping
beasts, still yupping, into low earth orbit, or at least well
down the block, but preferably into low earth orbit. Lester
wondered this long before the current Inane XXXXXXX Puppies
business; you must admit that such a device would be particularly
useful now and that Lester would have been a welcome pioneer had
such a device been developed.

In the absence of a dogapult, (the unfortunate absence of a
dogapult) Lester figures that the whole puppies thing is typical
of annoying canines. Lots of noise, sniffing of pack leaders'
asses, and pissing onXXXXXXXXXXXXXXXXXXXXXXXXX the local fire
hydrant. Sure, Lester finds their antics irritating, but really.
One Lester year. Seven puppy years. The puppies will be old,
gone, put down, dead, and no longer a nuisance. Soon enough.

Inconsiderate puppy owners sometimes poop on Lester's lawn. Well,
it's the puppies that do the pooping, but it's the owners that
aren't scooping. Lester rightfully grumbles while cleaning up
these messes, but it's also the case that when you have dogshit
on your lawn you got to clean it up. You can grumble about it,
start a neighbourhood vendetta, or you can just pick it up and
put it in the green bin and go about your day. It's dogshit, not
the second coming of Spanish Inquisition, and your outrage is
better directed to more productive channels.

Paying attention to these SF Puppies could be seen as XXXXX
XXXXXXXXXXXXXXXX enabling them, Lester would agree. There has to
be a bit of cleaning up and putting in the smeelly bin, true; but
like picking up dogshit on the lawn does not exactly enable
dogshit, but it gets rid of it. Otherwise where would Lester's
lawn be?

The Inane Puppies are leaving dogshit everywhere, as a mark of
their 'greatness' and 'brilliance'. It's just dogshit, as is
their 'cause'. Put it into the green bin and move on.

Flogging a Dead Trekkie: Puppies; the Sad, the Rabid, and Otherwise.

Neil Jamieson-Williams

Ah, Puppygate...

If you have read Thrashing Trufen: The Hugo Awards... (a few pages back in this issue) and you are up on the whole Puppygate brouhaha, you might have noticed that there is some resonance with the general position of the Sad Puppies. That the core active fans who are the movers and shakers behind the Hugo Awards nominations and voting are just a small segment of the SF & F audience. The claim that the tail is wagging the dog is, indeed, a valid one.

So, yes; I agree that the usual core fans of old style fandom are over-represented in the nominations for and the actual voting for the Hugo Awards. I also agree that efforts should be made to reach out to the wider audience of SF & F and get them involved in the nominating and voting process -- it would give more legitimacy to the Hugo Awards.

As for the sacred rules that the Sad Puppies are breaking[5]; SWILL breaks #3 all the time and on occasion breaks #2 and has, yet to break rule #1 (maybe next year...). The general analysis of the situation fits very well with what has appeared in SWILL since the first issue, waaay back in 1981. I can even agree with the demand that there should be new Hugo categories for Best SF & F Game, and Best Tie-In Novel[6]. I agree that fandom is fragmented

---

[5] RULE #1: thou shalt not publicly campaign. RULE #2: thou shalt not publicly point out blind spots or biases in the voting body. RULE #3: thou shalt not publicly criticize Worldcon or fandom proper.
[6] It would seem that the Sad Puppies leadership is a little inconsistent here on this demand; I am only infavour of creating a new category of Best Tie-In Novel, NOT permitting media tie-in novels to compete in the category Best Novel which must remain for works of original fiction.

into numerous subgenres and subsubgenres and that this is not a
bad thing.

Where I part company with the Sad Puppies is their claim that SF
& F, as nominated by the fannish elite, tends to be literary,
academic, boring, and leftist. And that this fannish elite are a
bunch of lefty, pinko, LGBT, anti-American, anti-capitalist,
feminist, anti-white, slackers, and "social justice warriors".
Wrong on both counts.

Let's jump back in time to the 2010 Hugo Awards for Best Novel;
of these six finalists, only two (The City & The City by China
Miéville and Palimpsest by Catherynne M. Valente) could be
accused of the "crime" of being literary - the Miéville book
commits the further sins of also being "cerebral" and requiring
thought on the part of the reader. All six are guilty of having
ethnic or multicultural themes (the novels do not take place in a
segregated "whites only" gated universe). All six, though two to
a lesser extent, are guilty of having female themes (the novels
take place in universes where women have roles other than wife,
mother, servant, sex toy) and one novel is overtly anti-rape
(this position is supposedly a bad thing in Puppyland). Two of
the novels have GLBT themes in that major characters are GLBT and
still people (which to the Puppies is wrong and immoral). One of
the novels has a protagonist who is disabled (lefty political
correctness according to Puppies). Three of the novels are
dystopian and two present corporatism in negative light (another
intolerable act in the eyes of the Puppies); one goes so far as
to be against Christian Falangism/Christian Fundamentalist
theocracy. Five of the six novels can be said to be fast-paced,
plot driven novels (even the literary and cerebral one), and half
of the novels are adventure novels. If one is not a Puppy, there
is really nothing wrong here, nor is this evidence of an evil
leftist, GLBT, feminist plot to pervert the precious bodily
fluids of SF & F on the part of the fannish elite (unless the
only SF & F you like are things like the Gor series of novels).

Leaping forward in time from 2010 to 2013 - prior to there being
any official Puppy slate, and this is supposedly what sparked the
Puppy outrage - I see nothing within the five nominees for Best
Novel that should upset the Puppies. Two of the five novels are

space opera (something the Puppies seem to like) and one is a
heroic fantasy (something the Puppies also like). However, two
of the five novels do have ethnic themes, and four of the five
have strong female themes, one has minor GLBT themes, and one has
non-Christian religious themes. In addition one novel (2312 by
Kim Stanley Robinson) is actually gender neutral, in that within
the universe of the novel, gender is optional and fluid;
government is also anarchic in structure (counter to the tastes
of the Puppies who prefer genders to be strictly defined and
their governments top-down -- authoritarian capitalist with
perhaps a veneer of democracy); this novel makes the further sin
of being slow paced and low on action-adventure. Nevertheless,
there is little here to be upset about.

As for the claim that the fannish elite are a bunch of "social
justice warriors", I have one question for the Puppies; have you
even attended a fan-run SF & F convention (not a trade show
convention like FanExpo or ComicCon)? Because, if you have, you
would know that the fannish elite that you are dissing - the
people who attend fan-run conventions like Ad Astra, tend to be
predominantly over thirty (most over forty), male, and of
European descent (i.e. white). And if you are really looking for
the fannish elite, a convention like SFContario is more
representative - even an older average age, even more male, and
even more white - and it is the type of fan who attends cons like
SFContario who are more frequently the type of fan who
participates in the nomination and voting for the Hugos. I can
tell you one thing, although many these fans often behave like an
elite, though they often can engage in exclusive behaviour, they
come in a wide variety of political stripes and leftist is
nowhere near the dominant one (of course, if your politics are
that of the USA Tea Party - i.e. three quarters of the way down
the road to being a full fascist - then even most of the USA
Republian party is leftist to you).

The fannish elite, (an elite only because they habitually
nominate and vote for the Hugo Awards, even though they are just
a small segment of the entire SF & F audience) can be swayed by
campaigning. The Puppies are correct, they have not broken any
rules and campaigning occurs all the time with the Hugos;
however, this promotion (via room parties with well stocked open

bars, convention giveaways, etc.) has normally been done by authors or publishers. It kind of goes hand-in-hand with any awards, and this, more than any Puppy conspiracy theory, has a major impact as to what get nominated, in the print medium, for the Hugos - the fannish elite place far more emphasis on the print medium than the Puppies do. And the Puppies, based on their own diatribes, place greater emphasis on gaming, media tie-ins, internet media, and audio-visual media.

The prescription offered by the Sad Puppies, is absolute rubbish. They want visceral, gut-level, swashbuckling fun -- old space opera and heroic fantasy -- or Campbell happy engineer tales. But wait; don't the Puppies also dis the fannish elite for being stuck in the 1970s, when there were hardly any subgenres in SF & F? Don't the Puppies claim that there are now a myriad of subgenres and subsubgenres in SF & F and that is a positive development and a demonstration that the fannish elite are an unrepresentative minority? So explain why it is a bad thing and evil that one unrepresentative group, a group that often reads a variety of books from a variety of subgenres within SF & F, is evil when they (inadvertantly) control the nominations and voting for the Hugos and that it is good thing and wonderful that another unrepresentative group (the Puppies), a group that only read works within a narrow set of interrelated subgenres, has intentionally taken over the Hugo nominations? It is not logical or rational. The phrase shit for brains comes to mind. This may be the Sad Puppies idea of a solution; it is not mine.

If the Sad Puppies are problematic (I do agree with much of the Sad Puppies general criticism, just not their final analysis nor their solution), the Rabid Puppies are just that -- rabid and crazy. While there is the undertone in the Sad Puppies that longs for pure adventure fiction, where the hero is always good and right, and that he will always be able to solve the dilemmas he encounters with the aid of capitalism, pull-yourself-up-by-your-own-bootstraps ethics, and the Imperial Galactic Fleet, etcetera, etcetera, etcetera... In the Rabid Puppies, it is not and undertone, it is overt and in your face. SF must be pro-capitalism, pro-Christian fundamentalism or pro-Christian fundamentalist theocracy, libertarian for the right sort of people and authoritarian dictatorship for the wrong sort of people (women, non-whites, LGBT people, non-Christians, leftists, etc.). There is a term for this; Christian Falangism -- i.e. Christian Fascism. And the Rabid Puppies are just a pack of feral, nasty thugs (whch kind of goes with being a fascist) who should be treated as one treats any rabid animal.

The Worldcon better fix things. Yes, we should see some additional categories (I would also add that there should be a category for Best YA Novel) and yes, we should try and make the average member of the SF & F audience aware of how they can participate in the nomination and voting process. But something has to be done regarding slates and block voting, otherwise there will be a horde of slates, from all kinds of groups, each with their own agendas. I don't care for either of the two Puppies. There should be no Puppies, period. I would, personally, like to see Dead Puppies.

Scribbling on the Bog Wall
Letters of Comment

Neil Jamieson-Williams

As I write this, there is one LoC from the usual suspect (Lloyd)
who was kind enough to rush me a LoC of SWILL 26 in time for #27
to come out Ad Astra weekend -- that didn't happen. I have had
some reviews of SWILL arrive since then, but I will save them for
next issue... My comments are, of course, in glorious
pudmonkey.

1706-24 Eva Rd.
Etobicoke, ON
M9C 2B2

April 3, 2015

Dear Neil:

Many thanks for Swill 26! Here I am, the Usual Suspect, ready to deal with
Pudmonkey in the Locol, and probably be the only one there. Hope not, but
we're all less active and more passive these days. Delve in…

It would seem that more people actually read SWILL than ever review
or comment on the zine. SWILL did make the ballot at CorFlu...
However, thank you as always for your comments, and the quick
turnaround.

Science fiction is the literature of ideas…well, that was probably true
once. The ideas seemed to be in limited number, and now, we may be at
bottom, and any ideas that were fresh at one point are now well beyond their
Best Before date. Newer ideas are what we need, something new that catches
our imaginations instead of something that seems dated and clichéd. Rob
Sawyer once said that SF was a 20th-century phenomenon, and he is sounding
awfully prophetic.

I agree with Rob, and yourself; SF may fade as a distinct genre as our ordinary and mundane world becomes more and more science fictional. We will see, SF has a poor record at actual prophecy...

Yet, there are 3D printers now available that remind me of SFnal tropes like replicators and 3D fax machines. If everything was printable, we'd have patterns for everything, and all we'd need is someone to feed the raw materials in the back end. Literally having cheap anything like this means it will lose its appeal, and the fickle public will ignore it. The future societies of SF look so distant yet so appealing; they are so utopian, and more distant than we know. We'd never set them up for ourselves because of personal interest on the part of our politicians; they'd need to be set up for ourselves, and guaranteed there'd be other ready and quite willing to tear those utopias down for reasons of money, religion or other dogma. Wish fulfillment is a fun read, but probably won't translate to reality.

It is going to go one of three ways: ~~dystopia~~ (nuclear armed gated territories for the elites and their support staff and the rest of us peons making do outside of the walls) and possible complete collapse (if the elites begin fighting amongst each other), ~~revolution~~ (when the middle class is more fully decimated and no longer sees that they have a vested interest in the system) -- though these can get messy and the new system may not be any better, ~~evolution~~ (negotiated societal change that is a balance of benefits for all segments in society) -- neither utopia or dystopia, though better than what we have and done with the least amount of violence. Not wishfull thinking, pollyanna stuff; actually quite rational and logical (though our governments and elites rarely behave in a rational or logical manner -- except in their exclusive own self interests) but the other two are more probable, though the third is the more preferable.

This literature of ideas kept us thinking, entertained and pleased when we were younger. Now, it's a source of good memories, but we're not readily reading more than what we're used to (I read mostly 60s, 70s and 80s, mostly because I am unfamiliar with anything newer. Couldn't afford to buy books, and never had time to borrow from the library, and somehow catch up.)

Just a thought, check into Scribd (only $8.99 USD/month). Kind of like a netflix for books, most of the selection is old, but there are also newer books too. An anyway, anything post 20th century will be new to you...

Reviews...I see you are a curmudgeon, doing some curmudging and being recognized for it. As you do, I admire Ellison's works, but some of what he says and a lot of what he's done in the past are up for serious comment. He's raked over the coals regularly, and he wouldn't get it if he didn't set himself up as a target. Bad publicity is still publicity, and it keeps his name in the SF public eye. He recently appeared at a meeting of the LASFS, and all were warned to be on their best behavior.

Good old Ellison. As I said in the Ellison issue and in #26, I do admire him -- I just don't admire everything about the man. Anyway, SWILL previously only praised Harlie-boy; he was due for a mild ~~shitkicking~~ tolchocking...

SF would like to be appreciated as high literature, and we know that it's not, it's good adventure for those of us who need a boost out of our mundane existences to experience (if only vicariously) an experience we'd never have otherwise. It's far from perfect, but it has served us well over the decades. I hope it is garnering new readers; I'll stick with the authors and decades I know well.

SF can be high literature, and in time, some of the better written classics will enter into the cannon of high literature. Just because it is written as popular literature doesn't invalidate it (Shakespeare and Dickens were both popular literature); it is the level of writing, the content, the characters, does it still speak to the present somehow. That's what makes a work high literature. Most of the works written in the literary genre do not last and are forgotten five years after they are published.

I hope this suits what you're looking for for the next issue, and I look forward to seeing it at Ad Astra. Our merchandise and table furnishings are ready to go, we're relaxing during the Easter long weekend so we can be charged up for Ad Astra. We will see you there.

Thanks again for rushing this off to me. Had a great time at Ad Astra

Endnote: The SWILL's Annual Message

the Grand PoohBah and Lord of all SWILL
Neil Jamieson-Williams

Benighted subjects and fannish riff-raff... 2014 has come and gone. Just another year... Nothing spectacular or too horrifying; the regular quota of misery and good. Same as it ever was.

Yes, there was the Crimea and Ukraine crisis -- but this is not destabilising and very unlikely to trigger WWIII. The nutbars of the Islamic State had a good year -- the sawing off of infidel heads and the rape and murder of women increased over the previous year. Whack jobs within Indiana, USA passed the Religious Freedom Restoration Act granting Christian fundamentalists the right to legally discriminate against LGBT people, Jews, Muslims, divorcees, Roman Catholics, etc. Arkansas, Mississippi, and Tennessee have passed similar laws(other USA states have legislation pending). There were the Malaysia Airlines disasters, mudslides in Afghanistan, major earthquakes in China, flooding in India, wildfires in California, and the polar vortex here at home. The circus act of Rob Ford brought Toronto international attention. There was an increase in racial-based police shootings in the USA. In the western democracies, security agencies continue to surveil the average citizen more than ever and with carte blanche from our "democratic" governments; as we, the people, become more transparent and our elites, governments, and corporations become more hidden and secret.

Yes, just another year...

Pith Helmet and Propeller Beanie Tour

November 2015 SFContario 6 - Toronto

SWILL

#28   Spring/Summer 2015

Table of Contents

SWILL is published three times per year: Spring/Summer, Autumn/Winter, and an annual every February.

SWILL

Issue #28 Spring/Summer 2015

Copyright © 1981 - 2015 VileFen Press

a division of Klatha Entertainment an Uldune Media company

swill.uldunemedia.ca

Editorial: The Future of SWILL

Neil Jamieson-Williams

A key editorial change has been made regarding the frequency of SWILL. For the next few years, this zine will be published three times a year instead of five. There are several reasons for this; time, relevance, and reader interest.

Time is the big one. SWILL takes up too much time that I could be spending doing other things. In particular, it takes up too much of my writing time. On one hand I have my academic writing; for example, I have a mid-November deadline for a new textbook, that as of right now, I am waaay behind on. I will make the deadline, but it is going to be a tough slog to get there. I also have about five papers that I need to finish -- no deadlines here, but I would like to get these articles done and out for submission (kind of similar to submitting a story to, say Asimov's, but with a far longer response time as it goes through peer review). Plus, there are two ethnographies that I also need to complete in the next couple of years and publish.

And that is only the "value added" academic work I'm engaged in. What I mean by that is that, within the Ontario provincially funded community college system (my employer), I am not expected to do research, write academic books, journal articles, present papers, or write textbooks -- I am paid to, primarily teach, as well as participate in curriculum development, college program committees, and other tasks assigned by my employer. And my workload has been increased (not just for myself, but my colleagues as well). Which means, I have less time available for doing all that "value added" academic work.

As part of the research project on SF (speculative fiction, with an emphasis on science fiction) fandom, I have started writing fiction again. To be honest, I really (and foolishly) thought that it would be a simple task to just re-write some of my old radio scripts. I was wrong; big time. Totally different medium (albeit closely related, but very different nevertheless) and that means that I am starting from square one with each fiction project. Oh, I have some groundwork in place with the characters, plot, dialogue already developed -- but there has been somewhat hard learning curve moving into the prose medium. So, I also have my fiction writing on the go. I am also way behind in my deadlines (at least these are self-imposed, but that carries with it the problem that it is very easy to abandon and/or reset those deadlines).

An issue of SWILL runs, on average, about 8,000 words -- the majority of that material is written by me. If we subtract the average length of Lester's column and one of Lloyds LoCs (about 1,600 words combined), one is still looking at the length of a longish short story, around 6,000 words. No, there are probably some of you out there who think that what I write about in SWILL is easy-peasy -- it's just a long winded rant, right. Uhh; not exactly. Usually, I have planned out the execution, some of the segments within the piece, quite thoroughly (i.e. I have done some research on the subject) before I actually sit down and write it. Most of my editorials and articles are not written in one sitting, and I do actually do re-writes and some editing. As I said above, SWILL takes time -- time away from writing other stuff.

Relevance is another issue. Lester and I have discussed this many times over the past four years. As I have stated in these pages (as has Lester, too); it's not 1981 anymore. Is there actually a place for SWILL today (Graeme thinks there is, but he is a minority voice). With the speculative fiction supragenre and the fragmented fandoms that comprise fandom today; is there anything that SWILL can say that resonates even with the whole genre of science fiction. Oh, we have managed to piss off that segment of traditional

fandom that call themselves the trufen -- but that is like
dropping a nuke on a cane toad. Over the past year we have
attempted to piss off right-wing fans, Trekkies, Ellison,
and so on... with only the briefest of whimpers from some
Ellison fans via Facebook messages (and the sole complaint
was having the issue come out when he was still ill). So,
are our critiques and viewpoints actually resonating
anywhere? Are they sparking any interest? Generating any
thought and discussion? We don't know.

Lester and I have also discussed that, in some ways, our
views haven't changed too much from the 1980s. A lot of the
issues we had with the genre back then, we still have today.
I have altered my viewpoint on mediafen from the early
1980s, but then, I have worked in media (also during the
1980s) and most of my anti-mediafen stance back thirty four
years ago was directed toward those mediafen who saw media
SF as the zenith of all SF in all mediums (sorry, guys and
gals, but not even Trek outperformed print SF back then).
So, one of the concerns that we have is the question;
haven't we really said all of this before? Is it worth
saying again? Are we saying it any better? And does it
really fucking matter?

Which leads to the third reason, reader interest. Over the
past four years, I have tried three SWILL blogs -- zero
response (other than spam). While it is great that Lloyd
writes a LoC for every issue, there is really very little
reader response. While I was speculating that SWILL had a
readership of maybe a dozen people (it would appear that we
do have a slightly larger audience -- see this issue's
Endnote) very few members of that readership bother with any
feedback.

SWILL takes a chunk of my time, we've given our critique,
and nobody really gives a shit. In the spirit of SWILL, we
didn't give a shit what you thought of the zine back in '81,
and actually preferred if you hated it; we don't give a shit
now either, except we do give a shit about wasted time.
So, SWILL will now be published three times a year;
Spring/Summer (out roughly in July or August each year),

Autumn/Winter (out around October or November each year, and the Annual (out in February). This will eat up less of our time, it will give us enough time between issues to look at what is happening in the field and comment on it, and it may give our readership time to draft some feedback between issues.

If our current level of reader response persists, it is the intention of both Lester and I that SWILL as of February 2019 will only be published annually in February.

And that is the future four-year plan (Gosplan certified) for SWILL.

Thrashing Trufen: Canadian SF

Neil Jamieson-Williams

Many many years ago an article appeared in Monthly Monthly (issue #4, I think - the front cover was on green paper and was series of comic book frames that presented pictorial instructions on how to kill a cat); the article was written by Christine Kulyk entitled "And the Canadian Way?". Ms. Kulyk drew upon Margaret Atwood's Survival for her article and related the Atwood thesis to Canadian science fiction. Way back then, I thought this article was fantastic. I have not read it again for many years - my paper copy disappeared years ago - and so any comments are based on memory. What Kulyk did was to introduce the Survival thesis and teleport it over into the science fiction genre within Canadian literature. I think that she did a great job for the time and others, in particular academics within the discipline of Literature, have built upon it over the decades. There are indeed distinct general themes within Canadian SF.

I would like to place emphasis upon the word "general" - as in broad, loose, and approximate - rather than specific or law-like statements. I am only going to examine the themes that I see as important, and there are people out there with degrees in Literature who will disagree with me, and still resonate (again in my opinion) forty years after Atwood published Survival. Those themes are Environment, Protagonist, Alienation, and Ambiguous Endings.

Environment is the big one and with it is humankind's relationship with nature. Nature is powerful, potentially malevolent, and uncaring - it is an additional antagonist to any human (or intelligent non-human) antagonist(s) that the protagonist is in conflict with. It is not something that can be easily subdued or tamed, and even if those two goals are accomplished, it is a tentative situation, a situation or condition that must be maintained, otherwise Nature will restore its balance, not ours. The image that Atwood employed was that of the garrison - a fortified stronghold, a safe zone of human civilisation - defending us from Nature. The walls can be physical, political, cultural, or psychological, etcetera; however, those barriers have a reality and do exist within the Canadian psyche. Thus, the environment is hostile and requires human constructs and modifications - our artificial environments[1] that we live within - for us to survive and be comfortable in. And those artificial environments are for ever under slow, pervasive, persistent attack from Nature. So the environment is a theme in Canadian SF; the environment is important, cannot be taken for granted, and can kill you if you make a mistake.

Coupled to the environment is setting, and in Canadian SF & F, setting and/or environment can take on the role of being a character itself. The setting may be a background character, it may also be a passive character, but it is an indispensible character. That said, this sub-theme is less prevalent in near-future/present day SF, but can still creep in. Robert Sawyer's Wake, Watch, Wonder trilogy is set within the present but the environment that emergent AI Webmind inhabits - cyberspace - becomes a setting for this major character. The setting and environment can also be a background character that is also an active character or antagonist.

That setting or environment is not only the physical; it is often also the human environment of our societies (including our governments and social institutions). There can be conflict between the individual and the collective that arises out of dependency and survival; the individual is dependent upon society while at the same time there is a struggle to retain their individuality. The rugged individual - independent from society as a whole - is a trope that has little traction in Canadian literature. That doesn't mean that the trope doesn't exist, but when it appears, this character usually is either cast as an outsider or as a well-meaning fool - Nature will get them in the end, unless they are saved by the collective action of society. Society itself is composed of different classes, hierarchies, and, in particular, cultures. The latter is a key trope - Canada has two "founding cultures", the British and the French (plus all of the aboriginal cultures) - there is no monoculture in Canadian literature (and if you create one, you will have to explain why

[1] The vast majority of SWILL readers probably live within one of these complex artificial environments (unless you are living in a tent somewhere north of Kapuskasing) that we call a municipality - be it a village or a city - that is an artificial environment that we have constructed and modified from Nature. The majority of Canadians live in cities, so the average day for the average person means moving from one artificial environment to another within the larger modified environment that is the city. Even when we go to a large urban park, it is a modified environment, not a natural one (it's just a bit more natural than say a shopping mall). We tend to live within environments that we have domesticated from Nature but which are not self-sufficient from Nature.

that is so) because there is no monoculture within Canadian society. We have always been a nation of multiple cultures in cohabitation, with some cultures and subcultures having greater access to power and opportunity than others - this is also reflected in our fiction.

The relationship between society and the individual and the government is also different. Rather than the government being an antagonist that attempts to restrict (and ultimately oppress) the individual and is, at best, a necessary evil - the American POV - government is seem as being necessary, period (though also remote and impersonal). Government may be flawed, it may lack all the information that it needs, it may have no idea as to what the actual situation is within a given community, and it may not even care about these failings; however, government is necessary and communities and individuals are in part dependent upon there being a government. Society and the government are not one-in-the-same (though they can be); society - the local community - can often be in conflict with the government (in whole or in part). And society can be in conflict with the individual or with groups of individuals while also working with those same individuals and groups; and vice versa. In other words, it's complicated. The social environment is almost as important as the natural environment and in literature aids in adding complexity to the fictional world and creates multiple sources of conflict.

Central point, this theme is important in Canadian literature (and by default, Canadian speculative fiction). Nature cannot be conquered by sheer technology and will (American SF) or set apart (as a preserve or dangerous area) and ignored (British SF); it is ever-present, can only be temporarily subdued and contained (if at all), and cannot be ignored (that path will lead to your undoing or death). In short, Nature is something that you depend upon, while at the same time, being something that you also have to struggle to survive from.

The second theme is that of the Protagonist. Canadian literature does not tend toward the classic protagonist - the hero protagonist - the exceptional individual who takes charge and initiates action, and by using their strengths (and weaknesses) struggle against the antagonist(s) and either triumph or fail based on their own actions. That is not to say that this type of protagonist does not exist within Canadian literature (they do), only that it is more common to see a different type of protagonist - the average person protagonist. The average person protagonist is not to be confused with the mythic archetype in American literature, "the common man". This archetype, while not a powerful person at the start of the story, is also not an average person; they are the exceptional individual whose exceptionality is dormant until actualised by the story's inciting incident.

The average person protagonist is just that, an ordinary person (warts and all) who does not initiate action, they do not become the hero protagonist in response to the inciting incident, they are just someone who has now found themselves within a situation of events that are out of their control and that they may not understand. The goal is not necessarily to win; it is to cope with, manage, sort, and endure amidst all that has been thrown at the protagonist - to survive - and perhaps figure out what is going on and find some sort of resolution to it, or not. This protagonist tends not to be a "lone wolf" and works with others in the attempt to achieve their goals - oh, and the initial goals can shift as the situation changes, and the situation is almost never something that the protagonist has any control over, or at best, only partial control over.

In addition, this protagonist is not only uncertain regarding the events that they have been thrown into, they are also uncertain as to their responses to those events. There may be more questions than answers and the resolution may not be clear cut at the end - this is on a continuum and some authors overall, and some authors in some stories but not others, provide more answers and resolution.

The third major theme is Alienation (also known as the Uninvolved Observer). It has been discussed within the sub-discipline of Canadian literature that this theme has its roots in our national inferiority complex, that we are unimportant on the world stage and, at best, play a supporting cast role. While it is true that we are a former colony of the British Empire, and that as that empire declined we came under the sphere of influence of the American one, and that we are not the initiator of world events but the detached observer of them. Okay, there are some good points there, that I have some agreement with. However, I would rather approach this from a different angle, that of Alienation.

The reason for using this term is that this theme manifests the concept of the Other - the outsider - in one way or another. As Canadians, we are alienated on multiple levels; in resonance with the first theme there is the garrison mentality, the alienation between humankind and Nature, the alienation between the social and natural environments, and that of the individual within those environments. In addition, we have the questions of identity and allegiance - who do we owe our allegiance to: the nation-state, the government, the province, the region, our ethnicity, gender, etc. and which of these categories form our identity? Or are they in fact, identities? This complexity in relationship fuels the position of Other, of being an outsider, of alienation within our literature. It also, allows us to take the role of the detached observer and engage in self-critique - the television series Continuum is very Canadian in this regard offering a cautionary view of a future corprocratic oligarchy that rules North America, this series would not have been developed in the USA.

Canada is not a great power or superpower, we are a middle power and therefore our position on the world stage is that of a supporting role (and sometimes reduced to that of a background performer). Our actual role is determined by the great powers and our ability to have influence upon them; when our influence is low, we are treated as if we were a small power (a nation of no consequence). Here we also find ourself in the role of the Other or an outsider, a role that we have little control over in most cases; again, the upside is that it can allow us to take a detached observer position. Our national inferiority complex is driven by the fact that our neighbour is a superpower, and one of our forms of identity is rooted in the notion of the Other - i.e we are not Americans.[2] Furthermore, we tend to, as detached observers, take into account the actual complexity of global problems, as opposed to ideological solutions (the current government being an unfortunate exception).

The sense of alienation, the complexity of identity, culture, roles, allegiances, etc. tends to result in a literature, and a science fiction, where the Protagonist often takes the role of the Other.

The fourth theme is that of the Ambiguous Ending. This is kind of a logical conclusion from the other three themes. If your literature tends towards the goals of enduring or surviving, and has a protagonist who is just an ordinary person - more acted

---

[2] Americans, Australians, Canadians, and New Zealanders, are actually more similar than they are different as these nation-states were all former colonies of the British Empire - and that means that they are also more similar than different in regards to the Irish and the British too. However, each has distinct histories and cultural divergences from the root cultures.

upon than the initiator of action - who probably has more than one allegiance, an ambiguous identity, and may be an alienated Other; ambiguous ending are not to be unexpected. Nor is the pessimistic ending, for that matter. One of the more interesting aspects of Canadian SF & F is that it is ambiguous in another manner as well; it is not uncommon for it to cross genre lines, as if the boundaries were imaginary all along. Science fiction and mystery, is the work adult or is it young adult or is it both, is it speculative fiction or is it literary fiction… And so it goes.

In conclusion, of sorts, let me restate that these are general themes that tend to be found within Canadian speculative fiction. Not all Canadian authors of speculative fiction deal with these themes in every work or all of the time. Some paint these themes with a very fine brush in the background and others use broad strokes with these themes, and others still make them the focal points in the foreground. And then there are some authors who barely touch on these themes and who would claim that they are not present at all in their works. And, these themes are also found outside of Canadian SF & F; they are not themes only used by Canadians, but they are themes that are frequently used by Canadians. As such, they serve to characterise Canadian speculative fiction.

<u>Pissing on a Pile of Old Amazings</u>
A Modest Column by Lester Rainsford

So you would think that there are lots of resources XX if one wanted
to learn about Caanadian SF writers. Lester thought so too. Lester
was wrong. On-line, there are some websites but nothing
comprehensive. Lester understands that this kind of work takes time
and effort, so it's not a huge surprise. But printed literature came
up short too. There are conference proceedings but the published
articles have a narrow focus.

What Lester was interested in was the backgrounds of Canadian SF
authors.In the nature/nurture balance, if, say, the mahjority of
Canadian SF writers are bicycle couriers, Lester would expect a lot
of gonzo punk SF stories. (As a fan of <u>Snow Crach</u>, Lester would
approve.)   As it turns out, the most- upto date collection of
Canadian SF biographical sketches is from 2004. Lots of Canadian SF
writers have an academic background, unless the writer is Quewbecois,
in shich case it's 100% more or less. Lester read the bio of A.E.
van Vogt with great interest, not knowing that van Vogt's early and
most influential works were writtine in Canada. Van Vogt did work
for the war department in Ottawa in the early 1940s. Lester regrets
that there are no secret Canadian moonbases in van Vogt's work.

Then Lester turned the pages to look up Karl Schroeder, who has said
that he was born in the same town as van Vogt. But, no entry for
Schroeder, which Lester found very odd because of the many entiries
for obsucre Quebec SF writers who published a couple of books in
French in the 1970s. Huh.

In 2014, <u>Ancillary Justice </u>got a bit of buzz and won some awards.
Lester read the book, and expects that Swill's readers have too. If
not, Lester assumes that spoilers are of no concern, because if they
were, the book would have been read int he first place.

What Lester found interesting was that <u>Ancillary Justice</u> is a book
that would not have raised eyebrows in 1986, and would not have been
the furthest-out new-wave work in 1968. While there is AI, and the
protagonist is a detached part of a group AI mind, the story doesn't
rely on XXYXXIXXXXHXANXIXHXAXHXXIXX any interesting explorations on how
a detached AI would think or work. The technical details are a bit
twenty-first century, but not startlingly so. But what Lester really
noticed XX XXXX the emotional arc of the plot. It's based on the
martyrdom of an important character. The importance of the character
is, in fact, contingent of the character's martyrdom. This
irresistibly reminds Lester of the emotional arc of many books that
came out in the 1980s. Someone gets killed in an unfair way, and
then that killing becomes the motivation behind the resto f the plot.
Lester thinks that books X by M.K Wren and such had this kind of plot

arc. But it was thirty years ago. So Lester is not as definitive as
someone who is paid to produce a 200+ page volume of Canadian SF
author bios (but excludes Karl Schroeder) might be.

What Lester can do is make a recommendation. For younger SF readers,
if Ancillary Justice was good, look up some of the good older stuff,
because it's going to be similar in feel. Read Delany's Nova. Read
Herbert's Dune and Dune Messiah--and stop there. Read Schmitz's
Witches of Karres. (It's not, in truth, like Ancillary Justice, but
you will have fun anyway.) Find some short=-story collections in
the second-hand stores. Kuttner, Kornbluth, Bester are all good
bets.

On the one hand, Lester found Ancillary Justice to be quite readable,
which is not always the case with SF works in the 2010s. On the
other hand, the plot was a bit unbelievable. (Lester is shocked--
shocked--that the plot of an SF work can be a bit unbelievable.)
What Lester is less certain about is whether a readable, relatively
short, and a military book that does not obsess over weapons types or
ultra-slow-mo ultar-violence should be applauded as a step forward,
when in fact it's a return to the good old days. Whether the good
old days were all that good, really, or not, is a big discussion.
But certainly these XNNXXNN are the current days, and what is current
day fiction about? Lester would find it depressing if the true
current fiction is in fact extremely long books XNNNX crammed with
time-wasting, page-bloating microaction scenes.

Then again, Lester can never agree when someone says "to see the true
America, you have to get off the Interstate". Lester thinks that the
true America is all the Dennys and Quality Suites and Wal Marts by
thge Interstate; that's where the people are and work and hang out.
In the same sense, maybe the SF of today is really today's SF. In
which case, Lester is in the market for a time machine. All tips on
how to properly search kijiji are welcome!

Some Shit Read: Book Reviews

Neil Jamieson-Williams

The original SWILL only had fake book reviews; the revived SWILL has had occasional real book reviews. Book reviews will now be a standard feature in SWILL (my book reviews, though Lester is encouraged to write some of his own as well).

This time around the focus will be on Canadian speculative fiction.

Among Others
Jo Walton
Tor   302 pgs
****

Jo Walton writes extremely well and her writing really pulls the reader into the story. She is also deft with the diary/letter form of storytelling. Among Others is a contemporary fantasy, that touches on elements of science fiction, that straddles the wall between fantasy and mainstream fiction. This means that it will not be to everyone's liking; if you want a plot-driven adventure, this is not the book for you.

This is a coming-of-age story and also a fairy tale. Not a Victorian or Disney fairy tale, but one that carries with it pre-industrial elements (harsh, wild, morally ambiguous) within an industrial setting, the UK of the late 1970s. The fairies are marginalised and shadows of what they may have once been, lurking on the edges of the remaining wild spaces and abandoned areas, vanquished and frustrated. They remain a source of magic, but only of one type of magic...

I like the magic in this novel; it has multiple layers to it and a strong internal (and ethical) logic. This magic works with the real world, is a part of it, rather than being separate or otherworldy. The different forms of magic and its connexion to

14

the ordinary world serves to reinforce the blend of fairy tale
and realistic fiction, in this novel.

Another blend is that of the storytelling. Walton was born and
raised in Wales and immigrated to Canada in 2002; her fiction
tends to have a strong British foundation with a Canadian
overlay, of ambiguity.

Overall, I enjoyed this novel and would recommend this novel.

The Salt and Iron Dialogues
Matthew Johnson
Bundoran   22 pgs
****

Fall From Earth
Matthew Johnson
Bundoran   240 pgs
***

The Salt and Iron Dialogues is a stand-alone prequel to Fall From
Earth, that was published simultaneously with the novel-length
work. Both are set in the same universe and have the same
protagonist. You do not have to read them in order; though, I
did, and I feel that the reader has a better understanding of the
complexity of the protagonist, Shi Jin, reading them in order.
However, you make your own choices. Both are space opera, both
are intriguing.

This is not your typical space opera, nor is it set your typical
British or American space operatic type of universe. I also feel
that this universe, while it has parallels in history, has a
strong Canadian favour to it. And as in all good Canadian
speculative fiction, the universe and the setting are not just
backdrop, but actually characters themselves. Both the novella
and the novel are set within the Borderless Empire - the centre
being Earth where a Chinese Confucian-Christian culture is
dominant. I have grumbled within SWILL about the lack of
cultural estrangement in science fiction - in these works Johnson
rises to that challenge. The Borderless Empire is hegemonic,
bureaucratic, old, and well established - it has put down many
rebellions/revolts/insurrections in the past - and is confident

that it can deal with any challenges to its power and authority. There exists a disconnect between the centre and the periphery (the colony worlds) both in culture and language (there is cultural and linguistic drift) as well as power - the colonies are definitely second-class citizens in the eyes of the Empire.

Entering into the Borderless Empire is not comfortable, like Peter F. Hamilton's Confederation universe or Vernor Vinge's Zones of Thought universe, it is a little bit hard as the culture is indeed different (which may turn some people off, but I liked the originality). Johnson skilfully provides nuggets of background that allow for the reader to learn the world while keeping enough out to retain some mystique. In the end, one gets the feel of a wholly developed, human culture, that one (as a visitor) still doesn't understand fully; this provides both works with depth and historical context (this universe did not just appear for the purpose of being the backdrop for the works).

Both the novella and the novel are strong, though the novella comes across stronger (I'll get to why in a moment). Both have good characterisation; excellent pov shifts between the characters, tight plot, that has a satisfactory conclusion - in other words, both are well written and recommended. Fall From Earth is a little weaker, in my view, because it appears - even though the ending is satisfactory - to end too quickly. I use the word "appears" as within the plot, it all makes sense, it just seems a little rushed. Again, this is just my perception. Nevertheless, a very good first novel.

Wake
Robert J. Sawyer
Penguin 354 pgs
*****

Watch
Robert J. Sawyer
Penguin 368 pgs
*****

Wonder
Robert J. Sawyer
Penguin 338 pgs
*****

I do like most of Robert Sawyer's works, and he is a gifted writer. In top form, he is brilliant; this is 100 per cent the case with his Wake, Watch, Wonder trilogy. In brief, it is a tale about a blind teenage woman who is a test subject for experimental technology (that works over the internet) that gives her sight as well as connexion to an emergent AI, and the relationship between these two beings - okay, that is really brief…

There is a certain amount of controversy regarding this trilogy; most from the disabled community raking Sawyer over some really, really hot coals for the sin of "ableism" and some from the same crowd who support the Puppies who found a disabled protagonist to be too politically correct. While I may disagree with Sawyer's technological optimism that is a theme (and he admits that this is a theme) in his works - I'm not a technological pessimist and neo-Luddite, but I am a pessimist regarding corporations and governments (especially the intelligence agencies and the military) in their use of new technology and who that technology benefits. I also would agree with Sawyer that if this technology was available right now, it should be made available to those who want it. And I don't buy into that post-structuralist worldview that any technology that would offer a cure to a disability is a form of ableist oppression, and all that shit…

Anyway, I recommend this series.

Red Planet Blues
Robert J. Sawyer
Penguin 368 pgs
**

However, when Sawyer is not in top form; you get this - just an interesting potboiler. A food equivalent would be a dinner at East Side Mario's or Boston Pizza, not fast food, but also not fine dining. I really enjoyed the novella Identity Theft - Red Planet Blues is an expansion of that work - and felt that the novella did deserve its award nominations (Aurora, Hugo, and Nebula). This was just the right length, I thought, for this SF noir tale. Expanding this story to novel-length did not improve the story; it made it weaker. Nevertheless, it sold well - so what do I know…

Elements
Suzanne Church
EDGE   272 pgs
***

Interesting collection. I am rather ambiguous regarding Church's
fiction; I have a binary response - I either really like it or I
really do not like it. All in all, a good first collection. I
give it a recommendation, though I would suggest that you also
check someone else's review of this collection.

Other Shit Recently-ish Read

Singularity Sky
Charles Stross
*****

The Sky Road
Ken MacLeod
*****

Iron Sunrise
Charles Stross
***

Newton's Wake
Ken MacLeod
****

Glasshouse
Charles Stross
****

Great North Road
Peter F. Hamilton
***

The Cassini Division
Ken MacLeod
***

11/22/63
Stephen King
**

The City on the Edge of Forever
Harlan Ellison
*****

The Science of Herself
Karen Joy Fowler
*****

The Human Front
Ken MacLeod
*****

Modem Times 2.0
Michael Moorcock
***

Raising Hell
Norman Spinrad
*****

Mammoths of the Great Plains
Eleanor Arnason
****

The Wild Girls
Ursula K. LeGuin
****

Flogging a Dead Trekkie:

Pre-empted Programming

Neil Jamieson-Williams

This column has been pre-empted for other content; the scheduled
column will return and its regular time and date in SWILL #29.

We apologise for any inconvenience due to dead trekkies not being
flogged.

SWILL

Scribbling on the Bog Wall
Letters of Comment

Neil Jamieson-Williams

As I write this, there is two LoCs and two reviews. My comments
are, of course, in glorious pudmonkey.

Amazing Stories
The Clubhouse: Fanzine Reviews: Into the Abyss.
R. Graeme Cameron
May 1, 2015

Swill (#26) - Winter 2015
Faned: Neil Williams. Canadian Perzine.

In his editorial Neil takes apart the sacred self-serving myth
put forward by many genre authors, that science fiction is the
literature of ideas. Oh yeah? How can that be? When science
fiction is solidly and comfortably middle class in nature (at
least, according to Barry Malzberg, says Neil). Said middle class
readers are happy to contemplate nifty near future gadgets, but
grow uncomfortable when the probable social consequences of
future technology made real actually impact economics (usually to
disastrous effect, as in mass unemployment).

In other words, entertaining ideas are sought after, but actual
extrapolation of current trends, especially technological trends,
is to be avoided because it invariably takes away from the gee-
whiz aspect of futurism and replaces it with the dire yet
inevitable consequences of technological advancement. Not what
people want to read. Literature of ideas, yes, but not of
implications. Science fiction self-limiting, in other words, if
it wants to remain commercially viable. Good point.

Neil follows this with an article showing how much of science
fiction depiction of near future society and culture is
necessarily bogus and unimaginative compared to what is really

going to happen. Again, reality is a lot grimmer than what SF&F authors portray. And there's nothing we can do about it (in my opinion) except observe what happens when it happens. So I throw in William Gibson's famous dictum that "the best science fiction is all about today." We can't genuinely write about the future because we're going to be blindsided by viewpoints and priorities which do not yet exist. If contemporary SF survives, it's going to look damned quaint. So I would argue that modern SF writers can either write thinly disguised warnings about today's trends, or just make stuff up for the sake of entertainment, knowing that it isn't plausible in light of what is actually going to happen. So, in fact, it would appear that science fiction isn't self-limiting by choice, but by its very nature.

Good summary there Graeme… I fully agree that SF at its core is limiting, by the nature of the genre itself and the pace of technological change. SF IS all about today, as is all fiction, really. Even a historical romance like the Outlander novel series, has been written in the context of the contemporary period (albeit the 1990s) and would be very different had it been written in the 1960s or earlier. Fiction is always a dialogue with the present, projecting possible trends (positive and negative) or pure made-up entertainment (e.g. Star Wars). And the projections always seem quaint down the timestream, like those late 1990s/early 2000s fictional tablet computers of 150 years or more in the future that are less powerful than today's iPads…

However, I think a better job could be done in regards to cultural estrangement than what we usually see. This is a balancing act, though – too far and you alienate the reader…

Which is why I always cast reality-awareness to the winds when I read science fiction. For me ALL science fiction is a "what-if?" alternate universe. Like-wise history books, or even newspapers and newscasts. We ARE a science fiction universe. An artificial construct. Interpret as you will…

Indeed, we live in a science fictional world today - another standard SWILL trope.

Hmm, possibly I've gotten a bit carried away with my chain of thought initiated by Neil's articles. I blame him. But he's got some darn good observations...

Thanks Graeme, and I accept all blame...

In his "Pissing on a Pile of Old Amazings" column (the title, I gather, is simply Lester saying he won't stand for traditional tropes) Lester Rainsford reveals that "Lester is a slow reader, and this makes him prone to thinking about the background and plot. This is never propitious to the enjoyment of the work. Complain, complain, complain-that's Lester's lot in SF reading life."

Seems he gets tired of spotting all the flaws and inconsistencies in 1,100 page novels. He much prefers 3,000 word short stories because "the author can put in a new idea, have a bit of fun with it, and be done. There is no need to come up with the enormous background information that's needed for a 1,100 page novel, nor any need to worry, over each of those 1,100 pages, that there's something inconsistent, either with the supposed future, or with the supposed future itself."

Actually, come to think of it, in the course of his article Lester seems to imply that the authors of 1,100 page novels are intellectually lazy, and the authors of short stories innovative, mentally alert, and stimulating. I'm sure most short story authors would agree.

Also, he wants to remind everyone we are not living in 1954 anymore. Well, he can speak for himself. I'm kinda 1959ish myself.

It would appear that Lester has elected not to speak for himself regarding your comments which were forwarded to him. That said, he may still address them in a future column.

In "Part 9 of 8 - Three Extra Taboos" Neil looks at the positive aspects of three loathsome and repugnant concepts most readers, let alone authors, prefer to avoid contemplating. The least offensive of the three is "Xenophobia as a species survival mechanism." In my opinion this may be correct under certain circumstances, but is liable to backfire if you happen to be the weakest of the species involved. At any rate, he has a bit of fun raising the hackles of readers, but then, Swill isn't exactly famous for its aggressive political correctness.

Political correctness, bah! Of course it all depends on context; from the Rabid Puppy POV, SWILL is in league with the vanguard of uber political correct social justice warriors, etc...

In his loc column Neil reprints my January 2 review of Swill #25. He points out an error I made (far be it for me to pass it on to you), and then says some very kind things:

"Graeme, thank you for your review and understanding (Lester, in particular, thanks you for noticing how unappreciated he is). What I always like about your commentary is that you actually get the concept of SWILL. And yes, SWILL is most definitely an acquired taste….

Of course, in this review I may have utterly disillusioned Neil in terms of my profound understanding of Swill, may in fact have bollixed up things considerably, but that's my style, wreak havoc and move on...

Swill worth reading? - Yes. Swill isn't shit disturbing for the sake of pitching manure about. Neil and Lester are in to questioning the basic assumptions regarding science fiction that most fans and authors seem to have in common. It is easy to be smug and complacent, but is it worthwhile? Especially when science fiction literature as we know it (or knew it) seems to be inundated under a tsunami of lesser expectations, overly-commercial formula writing, and a growing reader preference for fantasy over SF. In short, science fiction literature is in some danger of dwindling out of existence. That's a problem, methinks. So why not question the "basics"? Isn't it about time science fiction reinvented itself? Looking at from different angles, especially from angles totally alien to the three-dimensional universe we're used to, could well prove useful in rethinking and rehabilitating our beloved genre. Swill forces us to re-examine our values, our views, and our voles. (Well, maybe not our voles.)

Do I have any idea what I'm talking about? No. Of course not. If I did, I'd be a best-selling SF novelist wouldn't I?

Point is, I always get a kick out of reading Swill. It may not be to your taste, but I find it leads me to question mine. Keeps me thinking, it does.

Thinking and questioning, SWILL likes that (along with some shit-disturbing and nose-tweaking, too). Hope you continue to "get a kick out of" SWILL, Graeme...

The zine dump
No. 34
A zine about zines
by Guy h. Lillian III

Swill #26 / Neil Jamieson-Williams, swill.uldunemedia.ca / Is SF "a literature of ideas"? Not to Swill, which labels the idea a "sacred cow" it must slay. Rather than being a genre that confronts big questions and challenges common beliefs without fear, says Neil, science fiction is "a middle-class phenomenon" which conforms to the cultural norms of its target audience and seldom if ever risks anything. It's a perspective reminiscent of Fred Chappell's "Science Fiction Water Letter to Guy Lillian" in his pivotal poetic cycle, Midquest. (Blush, Neil; I just paid you a high compliment.) Following up on a piece by Charles Stross on "cultural estrangement," Jamieson-Williams opines that technology inevitably changes society unrecognizably - and that SF seldom follows up on this vital theme. Sharp and provocative, this Swill, far superior to the snarky-for-its-own-sake impression left by previous numbers. I even find the "dirty typeface with filled-in 'o's" tolerable this time.

Thank you for the comments (and the compliment). I am happy that you found this issue of SWILL to be more enjoyable and VT Corona to be tolerable. As to the compliment, there is not much that I can say — I have not read the piece and was only able to find analysis of it — other than I will track it down when I am back at work and thus return to it in a later issue.

1706-24 Eva Rd.
Etobicoke, ON
M9C 2B2

June 26, 2015

Dear Neil:

Many thanks for Swill 27. See what happens when you're away?
Someone let the Puppies in, they chewed on fandom and prodom
alike, and as Puppies will do, they've left a huge mess
everywhere. (The dogapult is a fine idea, by the way…) Let's
watch where we're stepping, and discuss this a little further.

Yes, Lester's dogapult is a wonderful idea. Even better would
be a Linear Puppy Accelerator (also conceived by Lester –
though originally for feline payloads) which would attempt to
launch sad and, especially, the rabid puppies at escape velocity
through the atmosphere; this should create a wrong-way meteor
effect for the puppies.

I guess there were plenty of writers, and perhaps some fans, who
thought that they Hugos were going to The Wrong People, people
with a left-leaning style in writing and attitude towards SF.
They also realized that with a relatively small number of people
actually participating in the Hugo nominating and voting
processes, it would be relatively easy to sway or seize control
of the processes for their own benefit. Yes, fandom has changed,
and will continue to change, and I think, not for the better.
Many fans I know who care about the Hugos care much less now, and
there's many more who haven't cared for some years now. Some are
advocating a new award, but no matter the rules and regulations
put into place, resourceful humans will find some way around
them.

There is one possible positive thing that may come of all of this rubbish;
more people, more fans, may become involved in the Hugo nominating
process. I have to confess that I have, not once, participated in this

process (though I have been involved in convention bids) and thus have had no comment on who was nominated and who has won these awards. I really don't see any evidence that the Hugos were going to the "wrong people", period. I don't always like everything that is nominated for the Hugos (or the Auroras), but most of the time I feel that what has been nominated has merit. I also have a different take on the awards than the Puppies do; I see the awards as being there to honour the best achievements in the supragenre in a given year, not as awards for most popular or most sales.

And I really don't see why the Puppies are all in a vile tizzy over Redshirts winning the Hugo in 2013 (this book was popular, it sold well, had a solid SF adventure plot – all of this should have appealed to the Puppies – and even though my personal opinion is that I do not think that this book merited a Hugo win), I see no vast conspiracy involved by the legions of "social justice warriors", just a popular book that won the award. It is obvious that the Puppy hatred is based on the fact that they don't like the causes and ideals that Scalzi supports rather than Redshirts not being in the same vein as the type of adventure fiction they support. Well, perhaps not so in the case of the Rabid Puppies as there are female characters who serve a function other than being a servant or sex toy or both and minorities who are depicted as being people – not permitted in the Puppyverse...

Traditional fandom, as you describe it, shoots itself in the foot every year. They complain that The Right People aren't on the ballot, yet, they do not go to Worldcons, and do not participate in the Hugo process.

Traditional fandom still runs the Worldcon and the Hugos as they are the fans who are involved in fan-run conventions. I know that others don't agree with me on this, but fandom of the 1970s and before, the fandom where the fanzine reigned supreme and clubs dominated the local scene, is the realm of the "trufen" within traditional fandom. The rest of tradfandom is focused on fan-run conventions, and blogs, and social media, and podcasts (and some of them still publish fanzines and are members of SF clubs), etc. General Fandom, by and large, attend trade show conventions, engage in a wide variety of social media oriented fanac, etc., and on occasion attend fan-run conventions. I don't see tradfandom or genfandom as shooting themselves in the foot, regarding the Hugos; I also don't know who the "right people" are as that is highly subjective.

(For the record, Yvonne and I haven't been to a Worldcon in some years now, and I don't think we'll be going to any more of them. They are fun, but they are a real money sink, and retirement isn't that far off. We do realize that there are so many unfamiliar names on the fan Hugo part of the ballot because, the most visible people eligible for those awards are online and contributing to blogs, and not fanzines. Fandom has moved forward, and left us behind. Fortunately, Canadian fans have the Auroras. When I see the Puppies' vicious threats and how easily they moved many of their candidates onto the Hugo ballot, I am frankly glad we aren't participating any more. And yet, I regret that we're not... I believe there's lots of people like that. They say the Hugos are shot, get rid of them, they're tainted, yet in their heart of hearts, they still believe in the silver rockets because they always hope they might win one. I was on the Hugo ballot once in 2010. No one remembers that because the Worldcon that year was in Australia. No offence to the wonderful people who nominated me in Australia, but few were able to attend, let alone vote.)

Our assorted SFnal Puppies aren't about to clean up their own messes, and most others aren't inclined to do the cleaning, either, so Puppy dropping are going to be on our floors for a long time, I believe. Fandom is still fun, but you're right, for the most part, fandom is male and white, and these days, it's in its 50s, 60s, 70s or more. Art Widner recently died at the age of 97. Fandom does have a proprietary attitude toward institutions like Worldcons and Hugos, feeling they've been willed to them by their predecessors, and it's up to us to keep the torch going, and stuff like that. Now, the torch has been passed again, but my own generations of fans didn't want to give the torch up, wanting continued glory and attention for itself. Not the slans we wanted to be, but we are just too damned human.

We will see what happens with Puppygate... Someone will have to clean up the mess, in one way or another. As I have said repeatedly in SWILL, tradfandom has changed (which is why blogs and podcasts do better than fanzines in the Hugo nominations). And genfandom has a different take on things and often appears to be unfannish from a tradfandom POV, though they are still part of fandom. Yes, the Hugos are not representative and the Worldcon is expensive, and so on. The whole thing will get sorted... And if it doesn't; then there is more grist for the SWILL mill.

I am still the Usual Suspect. This zine seems to have become a conversation between the Editor, the Main Contributor and the Only Reader Who Cares to Write a Letter. I am enjoying it, but still, I think we'd all like more than, shall we call it, a trialogue?

Yes, you do remain the "usual suspect" though I do get reviews from Graeme and Guy Lillian and, I hope, Chuck Conner. Part of the reason for this has to do with the fact that a lot of the people who remain involved in fanzine publication are also part of the trufen segment of tradfandom; i.e. SWILL's favourite fritz to tolchock. Hence, low participation rate in letters of comment. I strongly suspect that there is a large segment of fanzine fandom that hold the view that SWILL is not a real fanzine and that if they just ignore us, eventually we will go away and all will be wonderful once more. Anyway, we will see if the new production schedule increases feedback, or if it remains the same...

2014 was horrible for some, great for others. It was the first year in many years that Yvonne and I were employed full-time at the same time. Now, we are both full-time employees with benefits, and the last time that happened...can't think of when. 2015 has been a happy continuation of that situation.

Yes, full time employment is **good**; benefits equals even better.

We're having another interesting year...Christopher Lee passes, as does Patrick MacNee just a day or so ago, and now the rampaging shitstorm is rising against a far-from-unanimous decision about the legality of same-sex marriage in America, just to name a few events from a year almost half over. I'm just going to grab myself a big tub of popcorn, and observe from the grandstand.

Thanks for this, and have a great weekend...going to be making jewelry all weekend for our steampunk table. See you with the next one.

Yours, Lloyd Penney.

I hope that all went well at the various cons and events for your business this spring and summer. I will see you at SFContario in November...

Every issue of (the revived) SWILL I comb Bill Burns efanzines and select some new zines to include on the emailing list; zines that I think may like SWILL and zines that I think will hate SWILL. This is the first time I have got a response...

Subject: RE: A gift of SWILL
From: "Chuck Connor" <chuck.connor@gmx.co.uk>
Date: Tue, August 4, 2015 5:33 pm
To: "'Neil Jamieson-Williams - editor'" <swill@uldunemedia.ca>
Priority: Normal

Neil,

29 years ago I was in Vancouver - part of the Royal Navy Global '86 Sales Trip. That gave me a chance to meet up with Bruce Kalnins who had been doing Nocturnal Emissions. Somewhere around that time either you or he sent me two zines - one of which I remember being called (or so I thought) Mother of Scum, Daughter of Swill. It was a very chaotic time - especially with the likes of Tony Cvetco (Who Needs Life, I Get High On....), Seth Lockwood (Give Dog Boiled Yak) and something from Terry Frost (in which he also appeared stark naked on a sofa - a la Cosmo centre

spread.) At that time I was still editing IDOMO, bring in the likes of Bob Black from the US - and scaring the crap out of the established SF Fandom by spreading the zine across as many cultures & counter-cultures as I could.

Hi Chuck,

Thanks for the email. I think that we actually missed meeting face to face back in 1986 by a few weeks to months. It all depends on when the Royal Navy arrived in Vancouver – I am assuming that you were there as part of Expo '86 – as I left the province in early May of that year. If I recall correctly, I did my final segment with The Ether Patrol on May 1st and left for Ontario on May 5th of that year – as my EI (UI back then) was exhausted and the Socreds had reduced single male welfare to a level that would mean I would have to live in shared accommodation or a skid row room, and I had been accepted at Laurier in Ontario for the fall to complete my degree in anthropology.

Yes, I remember Bruce and Nocturnal Emissions, very well. Bruce probably gave you one or two of the three issues of Daughter of SWILL, Mother of Scum that I pubbed back in (see SWILL #20 http://swill.uldunemedia.ca/swill_20.pdf for a history of SWILL). Upon arriving back in Ontario, I did attend the Ad Astra convention in Etobicoke (on the border of Malton) and was unimpressed; Toronto fandom seemed no different than when I had left and at this point I 100% gafiated – until 2011. I have to confess that towards the end of my time in Vancouver, I was paying less attention to fanzines pubbed from outside of the city. I was involved in The Ether Patrol as well as about six other shows on CFRO, a couple of which I was lead producer for, as well as writing for local punk music fanzines, and being a political activist. In brief, I don't recall the zines you named; though I am certain that I would have enjoyed them.

Many thanks for reviving some old and very happy memories.

Most welcome...

For your sins, I've attached EAYOR #'s 2 & 3 (#1 is up on Bill
Burns' www.eFanzines.com along with some older shit I did in the
form of Detritus) + one of Rodney Leighton's zines as well - one
of the few people not to have a computer and still produce zines
in PDF format.

I do confess that I am a sinner and thank you for the attached zines. As
an unrepentant heathen of fandom, there is only a low probability of you
receiving much in the way of feedback (unless you mention SWILL in
the zine). I am probably the worst fanzine editor in Canada for getting
around to writing LoCs.

All the very best, and I look forward to reading SWILL - and
maybe some back issues.

Chuck

Great to hear from you, Chuck. I hope that you enjoy the SWILL back
issues as well as our current and future issues.

Till next time...

Endnote: Into the Void

Neil Jamieson-Williams

As foreshadowed in this issue's Editorial, there is some evidence
that SWILL has an audience larger than a dozen individuals. How
large this audience is; is completely unknown. It may only be
three times our speculated audience of 12 people, i.e. just 36
people, or maybe as many as a whole two score. Based on reader
feedback, we can only be certain that Lloyd Penny, Graeme,
Felicity Walker, and Guy Lillian actually read SWILL. Anything
else, is pure speculation based on little or no data.

SWILL is written, published online, and sent into the void of the
internet. Here at SWILL HQ in southern Ontario, Lester and I,
often wonder whether SWILL is released into a void or into a
singularity?

We now have some evidence that our readership is not as dismal as
we have speculated, though no evidence that SWILL is widely read
within fanzine fandom. This evidence comes from the FAAn Awards
(Fan Activity Achievement Awards) of 2015. Now, as I am not a
trufan and have never really fit in with the ordinary, run-of-
the-mill, fanzine fans -- I don't pub normative fanzines (even
when I edited the clubzine BCSFAzine, I tossed in oddball
material that caused unease amongst a segment of the readership)
and while I like the whole idea of fanzines, I also like to carve
my own path. Because of this attitude, I never bothered to
really look into the FAAn Awards or follow the results, as I had,
erroneously, assumed that these were American awards for American
fanzine fans. This error was brought to my attention in May by
Graeme, who informed me that I had "placed" in the FAAn Awards
for material published in 2014.

Now, of course, SWILL didn't place well, nor were we a viable
contender for any of the award categories -- but we did make it
onto the "board". In the category of Best Perzine, SWILL came
13th in a 5-way tie. For the category of Best Single Issue,
SWILL #25 (the Ellison issue) was in a 4-way tie for 21st place.
I managed to, in a 3-way tie, score 30th place in the category of
Best Fanwriter (unfortunately, Lester didn't even make it to the
board). I have been told that this showing is actually pretty
good -- even though the FAAn Awards are international awards
(like the Hugos) the voters are mostly American and the results

are skewed towards USA fanzines -- and that it is rare for
Canadian zines to even make it to the board.

So, publishing SWILL is not akin to tossing it into a black hole,
but it is similar to being a message in a bottle dropped into
interstellar space -- equipped with a beacon broadcasting "Fuck
you" on all hailing frequencies. Some people decide to pick it
up anyway.

BREAKING NEWS: Original SWILL cache discovered

Lester Rainsford announced to the editor that he had unearthed a
musty pile of old SWILLs with multiple copies of issues #2
through #5, plus a copy of issue #4b (the 1981 Worldcon issue).
With hope, we can get some better scans than are currently
available from these copies. Issue #6 still remains lost; I
don't know how many copies I printed up but they were distributed
equally between Vancouver and Toronto...

Pith Helmet and Propeller Beanie Tour

November 2015 SFContario - Toronto (real Toronto)

SWILL

The Lords of SWILL

Neil Jamieson-Williams

Lester Rainsford

#29   Autumn/Winter 2015

Table of Contents

SWILL is published three times per year: Spring/Summer, Autumn/Winter, and an annual every February.

Front Cover custesy of Hayden Trenholm

Back Cover by Fil Stiener

SWILL

Issue #29 Autumn/Winter 2015

Copyright © 1981 - 2015 VileFen Press

a division of Klatha Entertainment an Uldune Media company

swill.uldunemedia.ca

Guest Editorial: Sci-Fi Smut, Revisited

Rebecca Longspear-Jones (Media Liason: 1st Fundamentalist Church, Baxter, Iowa)

Imagine my horror, to discover that this unwholesome, purile, perverted excuse for a magazine is still in publication. The godless, editor (a self-professed heathen swine and anarchist -- i.e. terrorist) continues to purvey his vile screeds upon the world. It was bad enough when this was a small print run publication sent out by mail (and why did the US Postal Service not confiscate each and every issue at the border and have them burned, I don't know. I blame Obama, who everyone knows is a gay, Muslim, communist bent on the destruction of all that has made America great), but now this evil cretin has his own website that hosts the entire backlist of this foul, Satanic magazine.

When he was still alive, my blessed father -- the Reverand B. Jeramiah Jones -- did attempt to bring the editor and his degenerate cohorts to Jesus. Instead, his letters were edited, out of context, as is the norm for the leftist media, and constructed into some obscene guest editorial that these depraved parasites published. My father, I am told, sang Halleluhahs when it had appeared that this repulsive piece of dung ceased publication in the same year it was founded. But no, it crawled back out of the pits of Hell in 2001 and re-emerged in its full demonic incarnation in 2011. This publication is an affront to all good, clean, law-abiding, Christians in America (which includes the commie-state called Canada).

Has anything changed in over thirty years? Nothing at all. The smut that is science fiction and fantasy persists. Unlike my late father, I have not conducted any in-person research on the practices of these repulsive perverts who call themselves fans of speculative fiction (a true sign of their Satanic connections to the Illuminati -- the misdirection though using changed names for these heinious genres); there is no need to.

It is evident via social media, that the carnal sins of the past persist and have increased. Horrible as it was the sexual antics of the past -- orgies in bathtubs filled with lime jello, the wanton lust of teenage girls for middled-aged sci-fi writers, the depravity of their conventions -- this has only been intensified by the legions of legions of gay, lesbian, transgendered, feminist, athiest, leftist, anti-white, un-American, social justice warriors who rule this genre and whose sole purpose is to defile all right-thinking people, to corrupt the minds of impressionable youth, and lure them into the Illuminati goal of a one-world communist government peopled by the new "brown" race. Just look at the skimpy cosplay costumes, the furries (promoting beastiality), inclusion policies aimed at destroying heteronormity and God's will to create a sexually promiscuous, immoral, gay, socialist America, and the obliteration of Christian values.

And this dunghill of a magazine promotes this smut, filth, and heretical treason. You think that you are so smart, you SWILL people. Just you wait; when Trump becomes President he will crush your commie country. And if he is willing to act as God's wrath, drop a 1 megaton hydrogen bomb on the town of Dundas, Ontario, from which this vile publication is produced.

But please, continue your dance with Satan. I hope that you twisted perverts enjoy your eternity in Hell.

Thrashing Trufen: A Special Exception

Neil Jamieson-Williams

Frequent SWILL readers will have noticed that the editor does often peruse the blog of one Charles Stross for "burning issues of the day"; back in late October (October 26th, for the pedantic nit-pickers) Judith Tarr posted a guest column entitled, "The Future Is Not American". I was originally planning to add to what Ms. Tarr stated in her column in a reasoned manner -- however, some of the ongoing lunacy that has occurred south of the border since October (which up here in the civilised Great White North would demand attention from citizens, the media, and the various levels of government, is little more that just regular "background noise" in the USA) have altered the original plan.

The theory that the nation-state, the United States of America, is exceptional -- somehow inherently different, special, and thus superior to all other nation-states on the planet -- is a trope that many Americans hold very dear to their hearts. We are special, they believe, and it is our inherent right, because we are special, to rule the world, now and for the future, in perpetuity.

Over the decades, I have heard this shit escape the lips of Americans who politically sit on the right, the left, and the middle. It is a mantra, a dogma, that must be adhered to and accepted -- regardless as to which side of the USA "culture wars" a particular American happens to reside on -- it is an article of faith. In times past, I would argue this American creed, often using reason and historical facts to bolster my propositions and statements; but, why bother? Americans accept this belief 100% and there is no shaking them from it; i.e. one cannot use reason and logic when the other party's worldview is based upon unreason and faith.

So, fuck it; the United States of America is indeed an exception, is inherently different, and is special -- but, not at all in any way that is positive.

America remains, at present, a superpower; definitely this is the case militarilly and to a lesser extent economically. America is also an empire and empires suck (usually for everyone under the influence of the imperial power in question). While some empires suck less than others, the American Empire really sucks.[1]

At which point there will be many Yanks already screaming, "we're not an empire". "We have democracy. We don't have a nobility, or royal family. We have no emperor..." And so forth.

True, you don't have the trappings of classical colonialism and classical imperialism; because you guys pioneered and perfected neo-colonialism and neo-imperialism. Classical colonialism requires that the imperial power maintain a military pressence in the form of bases and a colonial administration -- there is some overhead to the extraction of cheap resources and chep labour from the colony. Neo-colonialism, developed by the USA, substantially reduces those costs (and, when everything is going well, eliminates them altogether); if you control the economy of a nation-state and in particular if you own outright or controlling interest in their key exports (how that nation-state generates income), you don't need that nation-state to be part of your political territory (thus, all the costs of military occupation, bases, and colonial administration disappear). And if you control the nation-states economy, you can usually control their government as well (most of the time). Thus, if you carry out a policy of neo-colonialism on a large scale, which the USA has done, you create a neo-empire. And the American Empire is a neo-empire and the largest that this planet has ever seen.

So, that only proves our point; we are special and we are superior -- we have the largest empire the world has ever seen.

---

[1] Now, I have been criticised, in person, for appearing too pro-British Empire; I'm not. In comparison to other empires of the same time period, I still stand by historical record, that if you had to be a colony (and no-one really wants to be someone else's colony) that your lot was better under the British Empire than it would be under any of their contemporaries -- it is still an exploitive relationship and you are still getting the short end of the stick and sometimes feeling a boot on your neck and it is not a desirable state of affairs, but it could be worse. Even in settler colonies, like Canada; two hundred years ago, in 1815, here in Upper Canada (present day Ontario) living under the British Empire sucked as your grain and timber (being shipped back to the mother country) was bought at rates below market value (set back in the UK) and all finished goods (from the UK) were expensive and there was legislation to discourage the production of domestic finished goods in the colony. All to the advantage of the imperial power. As the history of my nation is irrevocably tied to that of the British Empire until 1931, the British Empire is part of the Canadian context as well.

True; you have the largest empire that has ever existed. But
that is all.

But we improve the general standard of living worldwide and have
made the world more democratic; everyone is better off because of
the USA.

Yeah, there was a time when the American Empire tended to operate
in that manner, but only for certain people and only because you
had competition. Never has the American Empire gone out of its
way to actually improve the standard of living for the peoples of
Central and South America -- it has gone out of its way to
improve the degree of wealth extraction by US corporations
operating in those regions, but not that of the actual people.
The same can be said for the continent of Africa, where the USA
exerted less influence until post WWII. And any other part of
the world where the nation-states were not industrial nations.
In the cases where one is looking at fully industrial nations,
the American Empire has, post WWII, acted to improve the standard
of living and establish democratic institutions (Western European
reconstruction under the Marshall Plan and Japanese
reconstruction under the Occupation) but these policies where not
altruistic -- Europe and Japan bought American goods to perform
the rebuilding of their economies and infrastructure and they
also created cheap light industry exports for the American
Empire. It was also in the best interests of the American Empire
on a geo-political front; you wanted these nation-states to be
friendly and within the American sphere of influence and not
think that their lot would be better off within the Soviet
sphere. If, there was no competitor to the American Empire, the
Soviet Union, I doubt that the Americans would have aided in the
reconstruction of Europe and Japan; note, when the Soviet Union
collapsed, there was no Marshall Plan to restructure the Russian
economy and improve the democratication of Russia, instead there
was a combination of good old American carpetbagger and robber
baron looting of the former Soviet assets and the draconian
imposition of structural adjustments to the Russian economy, the
type usually reserved for developing nations with little to no
political power.

So, no; the American Empire only engages in the velvet glove when
there is an immediate advantage, or a viable alternative to the
Empire, otherwise, it is the mailed fist. Since the end of WWII,
the American Empire has invaded and occupied other nation-states
nine times and has, using covert operations, overthrown forty

democratically elected governments worldwide. In addition are
the numerous failed attempts to engineer an coup and the threats
of military invasion and the funding and training of death squads
to terrorise the populace and, with hope, destabalise the nation-
state's democratic government. Yeah, you're special all right...

And then we have the internal workings of the American Empire;
rising economic inequality, a racial-ethnic class system, an
increasingly militarized police force, a rapidly eroding middle
class, no caps of election spending, a two party system (that
from the perspective of the rest of the world are really only two
wings of the same party), no corporate accountability, an ongoing
war economy since WWII, religious fundamentalism (Christian),
decline in science and technology education, way above average
incarceration rate to population, massive and growing national
debt, crazy gun culture, polarised population, and so on... A
list that makes the Roman Empire circa 400 C.E look healthy.
But, you are not; you are ripe for collapse.

And yet, Americans belive that they will not only continue to
dominate as an empire, but that, they will thrive and grow to
fundicate the planets and the even stars with Imperial America.
Not bloodly likely! America is unlikely to survive to 2115
without descending into a civil war, and lucky if it survives to
2065 without having one. There will be no American Empire two
hundred years from now, or a thousand years from now. The future
is definitely NOT American.

For which we can all be thankful.

Pissing on a Pile of Old Amazings:

...a modest column by Lester Rainsford

Having put in over a year in a blue-collar gig, Lester has come to realize that there's a sad lack of blue-collar topics and protagonists in SF. All Lester can recall right off the bat is Gully Foyle in The Stars My Destination, which came out, what, 60 years ago? It seems that, in SF, our protagonists (assuming that they are adults and not Children of Destiny with no defined career yet) are computer whizzes or in the military or bartenders. This seems to be the case because that's where so many SF writers come from.

The implications of this problem have so gobsmacked Lester that he can't cover it all in a single column. There will be bits about Donald Rumsfeld's contribution to discourse; Piketty and inequality; dependence on auto clubs to get out of trouble; CEO compenation, and more.

Blue-collar work means actually doing something concrete, physical, in an environment that is industrial, or at least heavy-duty, as compared to office workXers who sit in cubicles, or retail workers stuck behind the counter.

The first thing that blue-collar work deomonstrates is that Things Go Wrong All The Time. Getting things physically done involves wear and tear and heat and dust, and that makes structures and machinery XXXXX break down and require repair. Lester is in awe of all the people who apparently will volunteer for a (cheap? seat-of-the-pants?) mission to Mars, when everyone these days is enrolled in an auto club so that when there's a flat tire the service guy will come around and fix it for you. So when something goes wrong, a hundred days out from Earth, the instinct will be to pull out the cellphone and call for service. oops! No cell coverage! All die.

Which brings Lester to The Martian, which is currently showing. Lester read the book a while back, and has no intention of seeing the film.

Okay, the book starts off by the expedition, presumably a major
effort, landing on Mars. And, ZOMG, it's windy, too windy, OMGOMG
abort abort abort. So everyone takes off, leaving the title
character. Lester was rolling his eyes at this point already. So,
no one had heard of winds on Mars? An inconceivably strong wind
comes up the moment they land? What, they didn't have a weather
look-see while in orbit? Huh?

Let's grant this piece of idiot plot just so the main plot can
get going. Lester did this while reading, after all. But the
entire book....well, the Martian would have been dead many times
over in real life. Once or twice, sure, he may have been able to
improvice, to cheat death. But one isolated human being, using
physical structures and processes in ways not intended, for days
and weeks and <u>months</u> and *years*.... Nope. Not going to happen.
The Martian is a dead guy, not even walking. Dead by a few peages
after the surprising weather. Not much of a novel, but at least a
realistic story.

But you see what's going on here, right? NASA or the UN Space
Agewncy (who is running this mission? Lester forgets) is
incompetent. HOWEVER, put a good ol' can-do generalist American
boy, and soon the RED planet will capitulate to Yankee know-how
and ingenuity! No way are we going to sleep under a Communits
ecliptic!

Damn, <u>The Martian</u> could have been written by Heinlein and
published by Campbell. This does not take away too much from the
entertainement value of the story, much as Heinlein is
entertaining (more entertaining than some of Campell's more
dogmatic writers)--while still insidiously pushing a very
particular worldview.

Don't listen to the amateur astronauts who will point to The
Martian and say, "see? a mission to Mars just takes some gumption
and duct tape! What are we waiting for?" Ask a blue-collar worker
if their section of the plant will survive a week of rampant mis-
use, XXXX let alone a year. "Ha ha, I'll be in the lunchroom
taking my break!" you will be told. You won't find the people who
actually do stuff volunteering to go to Mars. They see hard work
and broke-down machinery every day. They know not to trust to
super-complicated systems. And they are right.

Some Shit Read: Book Reviews

Neil Jamieson-Williams

New or New-ish Shit Read

New books are either books that are new, out for less than one year, or new-ish (recently discovered by moi). Very, very subjective, I know; though so are book reviews...

Leviathan Wakes
James S. A. Corey
Orbit   582 pgs
*****

This is great good-old new space opera at its best. Interesting characters, fast-paced plot, lots of action, and some solid science as well (I imagine there may be some handwavium in the novel, but no serious flaws that I spotted). I also love the fact that it is interplanetary as opposed to interstellar. However, this is a series -- a longish one from the looks of it -- so more on this at a later date.

I am currently reading Caliban's War.

The Martian
Andy Weir
Random House   369 pgs
*****

Okay, I already know that Lester hated this book (though I have not read his column, yet), but I loved it. It has been a long time since I burned through a book like this one. I was hooked from the first page and in bouts of near obsessive reading read the whole novel over a 72 hour period (during the work week). I had seen the trailer in the cinema for the movie, discovered that it was based on a novel, and then picked up the novel, not expecting too much. I was pleasantly surprised. As for the

movie; it was good, but just good (oh yeah the effects were
great) -- though I do have one question for the film-makers, "why
did you cut the fucking duststorm?"

My Uber Brief My Aurora Picks

My picks for the Aurora Award for best Novel are as follows. And
there is a bias -- I am strongly biased in favour of stand-alone
novels (or at least those that are initially stand-alone works).
So, that means that series novels will rank lower. It is also
why I support a new award category for novel series. But here
are my rankings.

The Peripheral
William Gibson
Penguin   485 pgs
*****

Best Canadian novel of the year. Typical future noire (cyberpunk
-- is that term even relevant anymore?) world with hard-boiled
characters, a fast-paced plot, with layered complexity and a
satisfying outcome. Really enjoyed this novel.

My Real Children
Jo Walton
Tor   320 pgs
****

Jo Walton is a writer that I really do enjoy; however, this time,
this novel, did not quite do it for me. It is certainly one of
the best, but not the best (say I). And, as reviews are
subjective, I think it all came down to me just not "bonding' to
either Patricia/Trish in this alternate history, alternate lives
tale (because, this is a type of story concept that I love).
Otherwise, well thought out worldlines and brilliant prose.

A Play of Shadow
Julie Czerneda
DAW   608 pgs
****

This is book two in the Night's Edge series. As I am not much of
a fantasy reader, nor someone who enjoys bits of romance and YA
crossover into their SpecFic, I quite enjoyed both A Turn of
Light and A Play of Shadow. Czerneda introduces us to more of
the well-defined world that she created in this sequel. The

11

major characters are strong and further developed in A Play of
Shadow, and the romance, wisely, finds a balance that I think has
an appeal to both the Adult and YA audience segments -- and is
not an impediment to a reader, such as myself (who tends to
prefer the romance elements in speculative fiction to be
secondary). As with the first novel, the magical systems are
well thought out, and very interesting. An ecellent second novel
to the series/trilogy.

Echopraxia
Peter Watts
Tor   384 pgs
***

The Future Falls
Tanya Huff
DAW   336 pgs
***

Both of these books are later books in series/trilogies and I
cannot do justice to either of these books as I didn't have the
time to read the earlier books, just enough of Coles Notes style
synopses to be able to read the nominated books without being
totally confused. Thus, I am am going to be really brief here
and just say that I found both books were interesting and
engaging.

Originally, it was my intention to have this issue out in time
for SFContario and Canvention -- this did not happen. So, here
we can look at how my picks measured up to reality. It is not
too skewwed, but different.

    1. A Play of Shadow Julie E. Czerneda
    2. The Peripheral William Gibson
    3. The Future Falls Tanya Huff
    4. My Real Children Jo Walton
    5. Echopraxia Peter Watts

Other Shit Recently Re-Read

Yesterday's Children
David Gerrold
Dell   1972
***

This has been re-written by Gerrold twice to fit into his Star
Wolf series (which I haven't read, nor have I read the re-
writes). Originally, an episode pitched to the original Star
Trek series, that Gerrold turned into a novel. The novel has the
aura of original Trek all over it, but a better and grungier
Trek, in my opinion. Not the Roddenberry sanitised Trek of
military starships crewed with boy and girl scouts, but a more
realistic crew of servicemen who -- if they had any choice --
would prefer to be somewhere else other than on this starship.
And it is a ship that is the dregs of the fleet as opposed to
being the flagship. To be perfectly honest, based upon my recall
from my teenage years, I didn't expect to get though the entire
book before bailing. Overall, it is actually well done military
science fiction and had a strong feel of realism. The only
irritants were the 1970s pop psychology that Gerrold uses as real
psychology/psychiatric theory of the future -- I am certain that
it all seemed more plausible and cutting edge back in the
seventies, but from the vantage point of the present, yeuck!!!

Protector
Larry Niven
Ballentine 1973
**

When I was in my teens I used to read a lot of Larry Niven and I
loved it all -- I mean really loved it. This is the second Niven
book that I have re-read this year and all I can say is: what did
I see in this shit when I was a kid? Yeah, there are some big
concepts here, but the rest of it... Nope, sucks. And it sucks
without me even bringing in the sexist and ethnocentrism...
Unless, you are under the age of 15 and male (or are still
psychologically under the age of 15 and male) this is not the
book for you.

The Man in the High Castle
Philip K. Dick
Berkley 1974 (1962)
*****
I have re-read this book because there is the television mini-
series coming out (which I have already seen the first episode
of). As a teen, I recall being disappointed with this novel and
couldn't see what all the accolades were about. Of course, the
reason for that interpretation was that when I was a teenager, my
brain had not yet fully developed and I still thought Larry Niven
was high art and stuff like The Man in the High Castle was
boring, literary crap (in short, back when I was a teenager, I
thought like a Sad Puppy). In brief, I have matured; this book
is brilliant, so well written, with great understatement, and
deserves all of its accolades and its status as a classic. I
would go further and state that it deserves to be recognised as a
classic in American Literature, not just as a classic in science
fiction.

Flogging a Dead Trekkie: Reflections on SWILL Past

Neil Jamieson-Williams

Lester delivered to me another SWILL archive a few weeks before SFContario. I now have all issues of the original SWILL #1 through #5 (including #4b -- the Worldcon 1981 special issue). As for what was going on post issue #4, there remains some confusion. An original issue #5 was created and sent out to Toronto from Vancouver, to be modified into SWILL East #5 and with an editorial from Lester to be sent back to make SWILL West #5, when the postal strike hit; the original issue #5 was never seen again. In the ensuing postal chaos, issue #6 was partially written, but without any material from Lester, Hoyt, and Stephano -- so it languished. Once the postal strike concluded, I received some material that had been posted prior to the strike, but not all of what had been posted to me. I gave up on the notion of a SWILL East and a SWILL West at this time too.

I used the one piece I had received from Lester, reprinted (and re-purposed) the first My Fame comic from issue #2, and wrote my infamous Americon editorial, and an Endnote to produce an issue #4b in time for the Worldcon in Denver. It was a small 4 page issue and in re-reading my editorial, no real ripping violence in print or true trashing of the Baltimore bid -- nothing to raise great ire amongst fandom (though many faanish types did not like the editorial one bit). However, the front cover was done by Fil Stiener and that indeed many found offensive (see this issue's back cover for a reprint).

It would appear that in September, after the Worldcon, I published the real issue #5 with the last of the material I had received from Toronto, with some new material by myself, and a reprint of the maplecon III slandersheet as the back cover.. The issue had a front cover by Vaughn Fraser and was eight pages in length.

In going through the recent archive, a question emerges and refuses to go away; was there an SWILL #6. I am fairly certain that there was, but no evidence has been found. As the saying goes, "absence of evidence is no evidence of absence." Enough of Vancouver fanzine fandom remembers Daughter of Swill, Mother of Scum as actually being something they saw or read; however, no copies, to date, have emerged. So, while I have yet to rule that issue #6 of SWILL was apocryphal, I do have to state that such a possibility does exist...

At SFContario 6, we again had a SWILL party -- the only room party Saturday night (so we again win the last room party standing award, by default this time). As befitting SWILL, there was the usual fair of cheap beer, No Name brand snack food, bargain crackers with No Name cheese-food slices, and Vachon cakes. However, there was also a real SWILL fan.

I was bringing more ice up to the room when I encountered Derwin Mak and, I think, Eric Choi (both Canadian authors)by the elevator looking at flyer for the SWILL party that evening. Derwin was telling Eric, "I remember this, from when I was, fifteen, maybe. It can't be the same people, though. There was this editorial about smut in science fiction by Reverand B.J. Jones and something of fan art..." At which point I interrupted and said, "Yes, we are the same people." I invited them both into the room and brought up issue #2 on the computer and let him relive the past moments before the two authors had to get to a panel.

Later on, Derwin returned during the party and talked about how he loved SWILL, though he didn't care much for the issues that had a bee on the cover. And I gave him a copy of issue #4b before he left for the night.

SWILL, proudly corrupting the minds of youth since 1981. And if our corruption results in the path to perversion, and the descent unto the depths of depravity as a full-time writer of speculative fiction -- then, we have done our job well.

Scribbling on the Bog Wall
Letters of Comment

Neil Jamieson-Williams

As I write this, there is three LoCs and one reviews. My comments are, of course, in glorious pudmonkey.

Re: SWILL #28 is now available
From: "Chris Garcia" <of Journey Planet>
Date: Sun, September 6, 2015 8:54 pm

Good issue! The writing's solid, but there was a tidbit among the letters that got me thinkin'

"I strongly suspect that there is a large segment of fanzine fandom that hold the view that SWILL is not a real fanzine and that if they just ignore us, eventually we will go away and all will be wonderful once more."

The strange fact is that Fanzine Fandom ignores a lot of 'zines, sometimes for no reason, and sometimes for good reasons. The Drink Tank used to have lively responses, and they died off. Journey Planet, when we printed issues, would get a fair number of LoCs, but that ended a good while ago.

Actually, right before we started getting the Hugo noms, I think. I know a fair deal of Corflu-type fans read some of my zines, Andy Hooper reviews issues sometimes in his zine, and Guy of course, but very seldom is there response. Although, I think folks may have realised that every without any response at all, we'd keep on the zines. I actually assume that very few people read any of my zines, so I'm always shocked when we end up on the Hugo nominations list. We've never done well in the FAAn Award voting, though. The Dr. Who issue of JP got something like 10,000 views, probably because Dr. Who clubs linked to it.

Hi Chris,

Thanks for the positive comments regarding SWILL. You are right, I would pub SWILL anyway, but it is nice to know that someone out there is actually reading it. I have never expected that the readership was all that big, but prior to the FAAn Award results, I was beginning to wonder if I was only writing for an audience of five people. I am also not one to talk, as I very rarely LoC myself...

Nevertheless, real world commitments have to come first, so I am keeping to the three issues per annum publication schedule. Thanks again for the advice and pep talk, and the nice comments.

```
I like Rob Sawyer's stuff a lot... right up until the endings.
He's not a closer for me, and I really disliked the WWW books.
Calculating God and Frameshift are my faves of his. And there's
the one about the hypercube (Factoring Humanity?) and Terminal
Experiment has some fun moments.

Good readin'!

Thanks
Chris
```

Most of the time Rob's books work for me and sometimes they do not. Yes, his endings can be weak. Still liked the WWW books, but that is the whole thing about there being different writers and different styles -- there are different tastes, even for readers of the same author...

```
RE: SWILL #28
From:      "Bill Wright" <of Interstellar Ramjet Scoop>
Date:      Sun, September 6, 2015 10:48 pm

Thank you for SWILL@28. In old age I tend to read stuff from
start to finish, pausing frequently to think about the text in
relation to whatever topics surface from what's left in memory.
```

It can take hours and I sometimes fall asleep. Afterwards, I usually go for a walk. Whatever I have been reading drops out of mind, which is why I rarely comment on SWILL.

Today is an exception. Issue 28 resonated on philosophical, social, scientific and science fiction levels. All have more chance of making progress (albeit not necessarily engaging people in informed debate) if their practitioners are rigorous and more demanding of themselves, especially in relation to the possibility of them being wrong. As I think you imply, much work in those fields is shoddy, vague and careless in checking details, to the detriment of Society as a whole and, in particular, our speculative fiction subculture.

Hi Bill, thanks for your comments. I am also not as young as I used to be and I also tend to read stuff in fanzines and then forget about it, or forget which zine it was in -- because, at the end of the day, it was only a zine, not a journal in my field. As I said above to Chris, I am horrible when it comes to LoCs -- it s very rare that I do so -- so I shouldn' t be surprised by the lack of LoCs I receive.

I was struck by one of your interpolative observations to Lloyd Penney's LoC, to wit, "I see the Hugo awards as being there to honour the best achievements in the supragenre in a given year, not as awards for most popular or most sales."

That sentiment struck a chord with me in my capacity as administrator of The Australian Science Fiction Foundation's Norma K Hemming Award http://www.asff.org.au/hemming-award-2015-shortlist.htm for excellence in the exploration of themes of race, gender, sexuality, class and disability in speculative fiction. The Judges look for well written page-turners that have something worthwhile to say about those categories of 'otherness' in the human condition. They couldn't give two hoots about the popularity of the book or its performance in other awards with a different focus. Some Australia editors, publishers and writers focussed on book sales have had the effrontery to criticise the Hemming Award judges for not short listing their other-award-winning works. To which my response is always, "What part of 'No correspondence will be entered into' don't you understand?"

I suspect that the Norma K. Hemming Award is Australia has some similarities to our Sunburst Award here in Canada; the Sunburst is also juried. The 2015 Sunburst winners for Novel and YA Novel did not even get nominated for the Auroras (Canada's Hugos). And I have no problem with that...

Regards from
Bill Wright

Unit 4, 1 Park Street
St Kilda West VIC 3182
AUSTRALIA

Thank you Bill for the mild pep talk and comments on SWILL #28. I hope you enjoy the next issue...

1706-24 Eva Rd.
Etobicoke, ON
M9C 2B2

September 17, 2015

Dear Neil:

Thanks for Swill 28. I fully understand about reducing the zine's frequency. Fandom is fun, but it sometimes gets in the way of real life, which pays for everything, including fandom. That's one of the many reasons behind us getting out of running cons. Good luck on getting your fiction published; there are so many different markets out there now, and most of them are online only.

Hi Lloyd, five issues per year was just taking up too much time. And I am certain for folks like Taral, three issues of SWILL per annum is more than enough. Thanks for the good wishes for my fiction...

Science fiction has changed a lot since 1981, or even 2001, for that matter. I still consider myself a fan, I guess, but fandom

itself has changed so much, I might not be a part of the fandom
surrounding current SF. Also, the literary aspect of SF has
gotten progressively smaller, and the heart of fandom today is
all about Doctor Who, gaming, comics and even wrestling and
in some places, car racing. You've said it before, and it is
still pertinent, but who's left to pay attention and be offended?

As I have said before, a supragenre (with new, cross-overs with other
surpragenres). What is the heart? What is the centre? What is
pertinent? These cannot really be answered anymore in the context of
the supragenre. For the individual person, the centre, the heart, what is
pertinent, is what you see as being the crux of the genre/subgenre that
interests you. Offending folk; that's another story (though I think that
many will find this issue's backcover (issue #4's front cover) to be
offensive.

I get told that the letter column is the heart of fanzine fandom.
Perhaps that heart is flatlining. I get bitches at because I am
the only name left in the locol of any given zine, and I get far
too many column-inches in the zine. I figure I am doing my part
by providing feedback to the editor or editorial team, but few
people keep to that tradition, and many who don't keep the
tradition either ignore the whole thing, or complain about what
they see.

Keep sending me LoCs, Lloyd. I look forward to them. I know that
there are some fanzines that no longer have a lettercol -- they have a
blog instead. That's fine, their choice. SWILL has tried blogs and
discarded the idea -- our audience is more likely to comment via email.
It is also why I use reviews as LoCs.

I had always wondered that once we entered what we saw as our
SFnal future, what would we write and read as science fiction?
Perhaps SF will be more nostalgic than anything else. What we
remember reading has joined the category of old skiffy, just like
any of the classics from the 30s and 40s.

Yep. All that cool stuff from the 70s and 80s is old shit now. And some
has stood the test of time, and much has not...

My loc...awards are great, and I have won a few. The feelgood is
terrific, if temporary, but I think I've been smart enough not to
concentrate on them, or let them define me. I have other goals to
reach for that do not include a chunk of metal/wood/plastic.

The steampunk jewelry tables we had at two conventions...sales
ranges from poor to nearly non-existent. We need to find
different markets for our merchandise, and if it doesn't sell,
well, we may have to make a difficult decision about carrying on
at all.

That is too bad. I hope that things pick up for your business.

The FAAn Awards are definitely influences by the fandom hosting
them...   Americans and Brits. The hosting convention, Corflu,
has been in Toronto before, and Canadian fandom offered no
influence at all. However, I am plesed to be able to say that I
am a five-time winner of the FAAn Award for Best Letterhack.
Maybe some of the people reading the zines only think I'm
an American.

I will pay a little more attention to the FAAn Awards this year, but no --
I mnot looking for a chunk of "metal/wood/plastic". I have
endeavoured to ensure that SWILL is on the eligibility list for the
Auroras (not that I think there is any chance that we would win, but if
we are eligible, we should at least be on the list...)

Time to wrap it up and get it ready to send to you. We do plan to
be at SFcontario, but probably only on the Sunday, and for the
Aurora Awards ceremony. Both Yvonne and I are nominees, so we
should be there. I will try to find you at your table. Many
thanks for this issue, and I hope there will be more. Don't let
it take away from you making a living and living up to
your commitments. I'm pleased to see it whenever it arrives.

Yours, Lloyd Penney.

Missed you at SFContario, but I had to leave prior to the Aurora
ceremony. Don t worry, SWILL is not about to roll over and croak.
We ve just throttled back a bit. I would never completely cease

publication -- that would be a victory for the self-proclaimed trufen, like Taral (very big evil grin). Till next time...

Garth Spencer
The Art of Garthness #5, September 2015
Reviews

Swill #28, spring/summer 2015 (Neil Jamieson-Williams; published three times per year), swill.uldunemedia.ca. I've never known quite what to make of Swill, or of Neil Jamieson-Williams.

Hello Garth. However, if I recall correctly, you didn't much like the original SWILL back in 1981 nor my time as BCSFAzine editor in 1982-83, so no news here...

Apparently Swill is some kind of academic project on researching SF and fandom, although his strategy of pissing off different writers and fandoms seems odd. As he himself writes in this issue, fandom is pretty fragmented, and any specific subjects (such as self-appointed trufen) are few and far between nowadays, so any impact is diffused.

The revival of SWILL is and is not (simultaneously) part of an academic project -- it is a form of participant observation with fanzine fandom (that's the academic part) and is also, just a perzine, which is the non-academic part (though, because I am an academic, that worldview does creep in to the non-academic stuff). As I have said ever since Lester discovered the first SWILL archive in the autumn of 2011, from the perspective of the present, the original SWILL was rather tame.

Indeed, Lester and I did spend a whole five issues attempting to piss off different segments in fandom, to no avail; and the experiment aids in proving that present day fandom, is fragmented into sub-fandoms and it is rather difficult to generate a unified negative response (unless you manage to manipulate the Hugo nominations...). SWILL is a perzine, and will have within it, whatever I feel that I want to write for the zine (the same goes for Lester -- part of the unwritten contract with him is that I print whatever he submits, unedited).

On top of this, he has a lot of academic writing, not to mention fiction writing, to catch up on (hence the reduction in publishing frequency).

Yeah, and sometimes one also spends a lot of time on a near pointless task -- like busting one's mental ass writing a new edition of a textbook to meet the publisher's deadline so that it can go to press and be available for students in January only to be told by the administration that they have decided not to offer that course again until January 2017 -- that one will have to do all over again to some extent (the textbook is for one of my Technology and Society courses and has to be constantly updated). Fortunately, the administration apprised me of this change of course offering in time for me to inform the publisher -- pissing off publishers is not a good thing.

From his articles it appears Neil is still going on about CanLit and Canadian Identity issues that sort of died out, in fandom as in popular culture, sometime in the 1980s. At one point he writes that there is little biographical information available about Canadian SF authors, which seems strange, unless SF Canada and its members really don't post such information.

Okay, this is not my field (English Literature), maybe it is yours, I don't know... From my layperson's knowledge, the whole concept of applying Atwood's Survival thesis to science fiction (and later speculative fiction) did not occur until the early 1980s and I doubt that this analysis died out with that decade (or became outmoded). I would like to offer as evidence, Robert Runte's keynote address to the 2013 Academic Conference on Canadian Science Fiction and Fantasy -- which I hadn't

24

read prior to writing the article on Canadian SF in SWILL and which is, indeed, a better article than mine (though I believe that English Literature is Runte's actual discipline).

As for your other point, you -- as have many other -- are of the opinion that Lester Rainsford is not a real person, but one of my old original SWILL psuedonyms. This assumption is incorrect. While in the original SWILL, the main writers used several pseudonyms (there were three main writers of content -- Rainsford, Hoyt, and myself -- and two occassional contributors. The point is, Lester Rainsford is not a fiction (Lester, we're going to have to do a selfie to prove your existence)[2] and Lester's web searching techniques for things outside of his field (physics) may leave something to be desired...

From his reviews and reading list, though, Neil is well read in recent fiction (Canadian and otherwise). It isn't like he's out of touch.

Again, I am not Lester.   Anyway, Garth; thank you for the review of SWILL #28. Till next time...

---

[2] See this issue's front cover...

Endnote: Barbaric Fannish Practices

Neil Jamieson-Williams

Last year at SFContario for the SWILL party theme we had a SWILL
Inquisition (unfortunately, hardly anyone brought forth any
heretics for excommunication). This year the SWILL Inquisition
called out for the reporting of Barbaric Fannish Practices to the
Inquisitors via paper form, for the examination of heresy and
barbarism and potential excommunication at the next SWILL party.

Reports of Barbaric Fannish Practices can still be made, just
send your snitch to: swill@uldunemedia.ca

During the SWILL party we did receive two reports, both from
improbable sources. I must have stepped out of the room for a
moment and missed these guests...

Snitch Name (optional): The Twelth Doctor
Perpetrator: David Tennant fans
Barbaric Fannish Practice Committed: Dalek fellatio

Snitch Name (optional): Donald Trump
Perpetrator: celebrity cosplayers who shall not be named
Barbaric Fannish Practice Committed: Mud wrestling between
Sailor Moon and Black Widows

BREAKING NEWS: Possibly No SFContario 7 in 2016

Lester Rainsford attended the AGM of the Upper canada Science
Fiction Society on the sunday of SFContario and reported back to
me the news that, as the concom are heavily involved with the
Worldcon in Kansas City this summer, there may be no SFContarion
in 2016 (or it will be a relaxicon). However, the con will be
back in full force for 2017.

Pith Helmet and Propeller Beanie Tour

Late April 2016 Ad Astra -- Richmond Hill
                 SWILL Party will be held

Zero Tolerance of Barbaric Fannish Practices

Report any and all Incidents to the Office of the SWILL Inquisition

We need to stand up for our values. We need to do this at fan-run conventions. We need to do this to protect vulnerable neofen and aging trufen from exploitation and other barbaric fannish practices.

Old-Stock fandom values require heightened vigilance in the wake of the insidious creeping invasion of so-called fans who bring with them their alien and unfannish ways. So heinious is this threat, so ubiquitous its reach and spread, we must be ever watchful when issues of "reasonable accommodation" are raised. Accommodation of whom? Certainly not the fannish majority.

The SWILL Inquisition is not afraid to defend fannish values. We announce a further Edict of Grace, and in addition, we encourage all of fandom to report any and all barbaric fannish practices. We therefore re-affirm our determination to excommunicate all fannish heretics, in particular those who are convicted filkers and other terrorists.

Reports can be made to the SWILL Inquisition during through the snitch line:
swill@uldunemedia.ca

Grand Poohbah Neil Jamieson-Williams: Chief Inquisitor

Executive Luminary Lester Rainsford: Chief Inquistor

printed courtesy of Vile Fen Press (content provided, slightly morphed, by candidates of the Conservative Party of Canada)

Puppyland   x Rabid Puppyland

#30   Annual February 2016

Table of Contents

SWILL is published three times per year: Spring/Summer, Autumn/Winter, and an annual every February.

SWILL

Issue #30   Annual February 2016

Copyright © 1981 - 2016 VileFen Press

a division of Klatha Entertainment an Uldune Media company

swill.uldunemedia.ca

Editorial: Revolt of the Reader/Viewer

Neil Jamieson-Williams

For the past 35 years, SWILL (in its numerous forms) has triumphed the reader/viewer over that of organised fandom. It is still the SWILL position that the genre consumer is important -- the speculative fiction supragenre (including the genre of science fiction) could not survive on the purchasing power of organised fandom alone -- and that the genre consumer is the majority audience. Up until the advent of social media, this majority was, largely, a silent one. SWILL has also held the position that the genre itself is more important than organised fandom; a bit of a no-brainer stance, given that almost all (the exception being some segments of the "trufen"[1] minority who place primary emphasis on their style of fandom over the genre itself) of organised fandom are also fans of the genre. SWILL has also taken outlook that favours fandom as a hobby (usually a part-time one at that) over that of fandom as a way of life. There is no change regarding these perspectives; they remain as core elements of the SWILL worldview -- though it is clear that these frameworks do open the door to being "bitten in the butt".

Yes, I am talking about the Puppies.

The problem of the Puppies (the Sad and the Rabid) -- as I stated last year -- is a symptom of growth and success of speculative fiction, coupled with the hyper-polarisation of the Culture War in the USA. It should go without saying that change in one area of a society, will create changes in other areas of society as well.

---

[1] A sub-segment of Traditional Fandom that attempts to preserve (within their fandom) the values, tropes, and memes that were dominant within fandom circa 1985 and prior.

Back in the day -- the 1980s -- in organised fandom,
virtually all fans were what I term traditional fans and
the trufen minority was a much larger minority and operated
as tribal elders (even if they were only in their mid-
twenties) and called the shorts in the fan community. That
means that there were methods of social control, those who
had power within the community defined who was and was not
a fan, what was important to the community, who the eeevil
influences[2] were, etc. There was a sort of unity (as the
print medium was the predominant medium) and localness (due
to expensive long-distance rates and very few people had
access to the internet) and regionalism that served to
create an identity for fandom as a whole and for local fan
communities.

So, if you have hunormous growth in all mediums for the
genre of science fiction and its related genres to such an
extent that you have to lump it all together under the
speculative fiction supragenre. Plus the rise of subgenres
and sub-subgenres, and a shift from the print medium being
the dominant medium, to one of the large mediums, and the
rise of inexpensive communications and the internet and
then social media -- you get changes in society and changes
in the fan community, or more correctly, communities. And
thus, there is no longer any unity -- other than the weak
unity that we all like speculative fiction in some form --
is there any collective identity, just a plethora of
identities.

Power has shifted and blurred. In most communities, the
power has moved from traditional fandom[3] to general fandom[4].
I say blurred because the borders are not hard-line and
tend to be flexible and there is indeed overlap. There is
also variation between cities as to how interconnected, or

---

[2] Such as myself - according to the Toronto trufen.
[3] Traditional Fandom: digital immigrants, place more of an emphasis upon whole
genres or large segments of subgenres within specific genres, fanac varies
but includes conruuning and fanzine publishing, some knowledge of fan
history, still see print as an important medium, usually attend fan-run
conventions over trade-show conventions.
[4] General Fandom: digital natives, place more emphasis upon specific
subgenres/series, primarily uses social media for fanac, they have little
knowledge of fan history, they see other media as primary over the print
medium, and they attend trade-show conventions over fan-run conventions.

not, the local trad fans and gen fans are, etc. The same
has happened in regards to gen fans and genre consumers,
i.e. this is also fuzzy and blurred. There is a continuum
from the gen fan who barely self-identifies themselves as a
fan and engages in very little fanac to the gen fan for who
a major aspect of their identity is that they are a fan and
they engage in numerous forms of fanac and have connexions
to several different fan communities.

So, it is the gen fans and the almost-fan members of the
consumer audience that SWILL has been an advocate for over
the past three decades. It is also these segments of the
consumer audience/fandom who appear to be the support base
for the Puppies. Part of the reason for this is that many
individuals in these two segments of the audience/fandom
population do not understand traditional fandom -- its
subculture and its worldview -- they are not "fannish" in
the traditional sense of the term; therefore, because of
this they are more open to being manipulated by a small and
unrepresentative segment of the fan population, the Puppies
(who actually do understand traditional fandom), with the
propaganda (drawn from the USA Culture War) that the Hugo
Awards have been hijacked by a small and unrepresentative
segment of the fan population -- the "Worldcon Fannish
Elite" -- who are literary, leftist, feminist, "social
justice warriors" bent on unAmerican Activities and a
conspiracy to insure that the Hugos are nominated and
awarded solely on the basis of "tokenism" and social
engineering, i.e. X only got the nomination and award
because they are a member of Y or Z minority group. As
evidence to support their propaganda, they demonstrate that
bestselling authors C, and D, and E who have written very
popular multibook series have received neither any
nominations nor any Hugo awards. See there is a "social
justice warrior" cabal...

As for the Rabid Puppies; I have no use for them -- but
they are a royal pain in the ass. Their fearless leader,
based on his own words, is a sexist, racist, ethnocentric,
homophobic, Christian falangist, who really likes to stir
the shit. While I can understand the desire to shit-
disturb (I do publish SWILL) the rest of the Rabid Puppy

worldview is repulsive and regressive.[5] The Rabid Puppies
are pure noise -- obnoxious and annoying noise, but just
noise. They deserve no further attention, period.

It would appear that the Sad Puppies, in their current
iteration, have as their goal to broaden the participation
in the Hugos and to "reform' the awards themselves. I
agree with the first goal and am lukewarm regarding the
second goal; though I agree that the Hugo structure has
some cultural lag going on there that harks back to the
days when the "trufen" were the movers and shakers in the
fandom. I am lukewarm regarding the Sad Puppies "reforms"
because I have very different ideas about what these awards
should be celebrating than they do.

Which, we will discuss next...

---

[5] Of course, from the perspective of the Rabid Puppies, I am a person who is
an academic (therefore, evil), a Neopagan (extra evil), an anarcho-
syndicalist *[American definition: some sort of commie]* (extra evil -- perhaps
more evil), who believes that industrial capitalism is unsustainable and
needs to be massively reformed or replaced (very, VERY, evil).

Thrashing Trufen: The Hugo Awards -- Revisted

Neil Jamieson-Williams

Well, it's that time of the year again, awards season. The Hugo
nominations are open and the Puppy slates[6] are being compiled.

Last year, I equated the Hugo Awards to the People's Choice
Awards and later stated that it was akin to being a Some-of-the-
People's Choice Awards. Although I am not making a retraction,
looking back at the history of the awards, I think a re-
interpretation is in order; one that is germane to the
discussion on the Sad Puppies take on the awards.

Waaay back, before I was even born, they began bestowing the
Science Fiction Achievement Awards (aka the Hugos). Since 1958
or 1959 (some fannish historian can correct me) the World
Science Fiction Society emerged, more or less, in its current
form as an unincorporated literary society[7] -- one that furnishes
the structure for the annual Worldcon. Part of that structure is
the administering of the Hugo Awards, Worldcon site selection,
and numerous standing committees. The point I am making here is
the entire framework of the World Science Fiction Society, is
one that was created in the days of rotary dial landline phones,
post delivery twice daily on weekdays, and when the average
attendence at a Worldcon was 500 people. It is a structure that
is very democratic, with a high level of autonomy (for
individual Worldcon concoms), within a governing constitution,
and very much a "trufen" design.

And it is a good design, overall. It is also a structure that
is rooted in the days when traditional fandom was really the
only fandom and when the trufen were the power-brokers within
the fan community. It was also from a time when, if you were
involved in fandom, fandom was like a small town -- you may not
personally know all the major fanzine editors, magazine editors,

---

[6] Not to be left out or outdone, and so that SWILL can be found guilty of
breaking Worldcon Rule #1 (what's the point of only violating two of the
three rules, one might as well break the complete set), this year there will
be a SWILL slate.

[7] There was a big fan feud regarding this; the first incarnation of the World
Science Fiction Society was incorporated and this created a major brouhaha in
the fan community. So it was changed to an unincorporated society…

the authors, the illustrators, but you may have communicated
with them in a letter column or just by regular letter. Thing
is, it was a small community and you tended to know of all the
important members of that community and their work within the
genre.

So, for at least the first two decades of the Hugo Awards, they
were kind of like SF's Academy Awards -- minus the membership
criteria, the rules that you can only nominate and vote for
these awards but everyone can nominate and vote for these awards
-- in an informal way. The average fan knew how to participate,
if they chose to do so, even some readers would participate, via
supporting memberships to the Worldcon. This is how the Hugos
received the reputation of being the Academy Awards of science
fiction (it also didn't hurt that they achieved that reputation
when they were the only awards within the genre).

The claim by the Sad Puppies that the Hugo nomination and voting
process has become unrepresentative over time is a valid claim.
Their claim that an eevil cabal of "social justice warriors"
control the Hugos is complete batshit-American rubbish (and
while it may sound familiar to Americans -- it's quite similar
to USA Republican Party dogma -- and to Americans seem somewhat
sane; outside of the USA, it makes the Sad Puppies look like
nutbars[8]). As fandom has grown and diversified, a large portion
of the fan population has become unaware of how they can
participate in the Hugo nominations and voting, which means that
they haven't.

As I mentioned last year, the "eevil cabal" that have been
"controlling the Hugos" are not some conspirator group, they are
just members of traditional fandom, who have always remained in
the loop. Remember, the World Science Fiction Society does not
just do the Hugo Awards, it also administers Worldcon site
selection and the process that leads up to the site selection
vote (the site bid campaigns) take place at fan-run conventions
-- conventions where the majority of the fans attending will be
traditional fans. To vote on the site selection requires that
one have a Worldcon supporting membership and a supporting
membership to the convention bid; if you purchased a Worldcon
supporting membership for the purpose of voting for a site bid,
that membership also allows you to nominate and vote for the
Hugos.

---

[8] Not sorry Sad Puppies, that's what you look like outside of the USA. Still,
better than the Rabid Puppies, who are nutbars, and only appear to maybe not
be so to folks living within certain parts of the USA.

Thus, over time, the Hugos have moved from being SF's Academy
Awards to SF's Some-of-the-People's Choice Awards. The question
is where does fandom want to take the awards -- what path do we
desire to go down in regards to the Hugos? The sides, when all
of the USA Culture War rhetoric is stripped away, really come
down to the interpretation of the word "achievement".

The Puppies define "achievement" in the terms of sales
performance and success -- i.e. what has sold the most or what
is the most popular within the supragenre. The non-Puppies
define "achievement" in the terms of accomplishment and
attainment -- i.e. what is the best achievement in art and craft
within the supragenre. These are two different views on
achievement; if achievement is based entirely on sales, then no
voting is necessary, the awards would be assigned based on
distributor sales data or website hits for the non-professional
(fan) awards. If achievement is based upon a combination of
bestselling and popularity, then voting would still be required
and the Hugos would move fully in the direction of becoming
speculative fiction's People's Choice Awards with no membership
fee required.

However, if we define achievement as being the best
accomplishment in art and craft, we have to move in an opposite
direction more in the direction of the Academy Awards (which
would reduce some of the democracy in the current voting system)
and make member categories, such as fan, writer, artist, editor.
Only fans could vote on fan awards, only writers on writing
awards, and so on; while still retaining awards like best novel,
best dramatic presentation long form & short form, best
magazine, that everyone with a membership can vote on. This
would bolster the prestige of the Hugos as well.

Another option, a typical Canadian compromise (which means it
will be totally unacceptable to either Puppy group as they have
publicly stated that they will accept no compromise only the
American "spoils system" of winner-takes-all and the losers-get-
fucked) is that we move to a two-tier model, i.e. we do both.
One tier requires no membership fee and would have a wider range
of categories (best LARP group, best fan YouTube personality,
best military SF game, and so on) that people can vote on (which
may also get the genre consumers involved); this tier of awards
would not receive a "rocket" but a certificate (this is done
with many other awards where the "big" awards of say, best
television drama, best actress, etc. get an actual trophy but
the "technical" and "craft" categories -- the ones that happen
on a different day and are not televised -- receive a

certificate or maybe a plaque.) The second tier would require
that the person pay a membership fee (at the current rate or
higher) and where there may or may not be member categories and
there are fewer categories and there are actual trophies
awarded; this would be the more prestigious tier of the Hugo
Awards.

Or, the final option is -- do nothing. The rule changes if they
are ratified would make it more difficult for slate
nominating/voting to game the system. The system has worked
quite well over the decades and is not broken. The current
Puppy tempest will blow over -- in fact, it would never have
gained the traction that it did if they hadn't plugged into
American Culture War propaganda and then linked up with the
Gamergate people, the Puppies would not have had the degree of
impact that they did.

The main reason why the Puppies will fade is because their most
front-and-centre, their most vocal arguments are nothing more
than absolute fucking chickenshit. Their big straw-man argument
of the eevil "social justice warrior" cabal that controls the
Hugo nominations and voting doesn't hold up to scrutiny. Their
factual argument, that they believe that the Hugos should be
awarded on the merits of sales and popularity alone may appeal
to some people, but it is only a difference in interpretation
and opinion - not something that is probable to initiate the
desired "to the barricades against the social justice warrior
hordes" response.

And, at the end of the day, I think (though I could be wrong),
that most genre consumers and fans actually would prefer that
the Hugos be awarded on the merits of achievement in art and
craft.

Pissing on a Pile of Old Amazings:

...a modest column by Lester Rainsford

Having sepnt last column trashing The Martian, an amusing if unbelievable bit of light fluff (with some libertarian unedrcurrents), this time Lester XXXXXXXX muses about another book that was good and thought-provoking, The Traitor Baru Cormorant.

Be forewarned that this book deliberately pulls some chains. Those chains may not exist in all readers; those will find the book to be boring and pointless. Other readers will find the pulled chains make them upset in the wrong way; those will XXXX find the book unpleasant and depressing with few redeeming factors.

Lester is also wary of the announced sequel to this book. There are many, many ways sequels can go so wrong, or at the very least having much less impact than the original book because the bag of tricks has been revealed once already--the alter reader is on the lookout for these tricks a second time. The last sequel that Lester thinks for sure was a good one was Dune Messiah. That was both a long time ago, and a controversial proposal as Lester recognizes. (Stop reading at Dune Messiah. Children of Dune would better be fammily-planned, if you know what Lester means. As for Grape Juice Coolaid of Dune, it almost doesn't amtter which Herbert wrote it, with or without the Anderson. Avoid.)

Anyway, for many readers, The Traitor will, in kind of a summary of lots of reviews, yank out your internal organs, puree' them, feed them to rabid racoons, who will then be run over by a garbage truck. The garbage truck, skidding on racocon entrails, will nail you against the wall of a KFC where you will expire in the stench of deep-fried chicken.

Or something like that.

So it's not a book for Mercedes Lackey fans, thinks Lester.

If you read this book, pay attention to any possible inconsistencies that don't make sense.

The real story of the book is <u>How Do You Fight The Man.</u> That is of course harder than is portrayed in escapist fantasy or Baen (TM) rebelling-against-statist-control-brave=-free-men. The proposition is that it may be better to fight The Man from inside The Man's Offices. May be <u>better</u>--but does it <u>work</u>? It's easy to be pessismistic. Will the new FIFA president fix the problems left by Sepp Blatter (who Lester, juvenile-ly, thinks of as "septic bladder")? Ha ha, sure, and unicorns and rainbows are available at the local 7-11 (extra cost for unicorn-flavoured hot dogs).

On the other hand, Canadians decided that they did not care for Voldemort to be running the countryt, and elected Trudeau <u>fils</u>, who seemes to come with unicorns and rainbows by default. Will the unicorns and rainbows persist, or will they be snapped up by hyenas and a brisk sleety wind from the west? Time will tell.

Somewhat more parochiallyXXXXXXXXX. Well Toronto is the Centre of the Universe and Ontario surrounds Toronto, so Ontario doings are in fact of import to the whole entire universe, so forget 'parochially'. In the last Onatrio election, Kathleen Wynne seemed to be the only good choice, and a relatively promising one. These days, while Lester holds to the first part of that proposition, the second part is getting harder to concede.

So that is one big reason why Lester fears the sequel to <u>Baru Cormorant.</u> But he will readi it anyway.

What are you waiting for?

Some Shit Read: Book Reviews

Neil Jamieson-Williams

The Expanse series

I am not a big fan of series, most don't hold me as far as The
Expanse series has, and I almost always am late joining in. In
the case of The Expanse novels, this was an advantage, as there
were five books already out, and no waiting required.

Caliban's War
James S. A. Corey
Orbit   595 pgs
*****

Abbadon's Gate
James S. A. Corey
Orbit   539 pgs
****

The continuing adventures of the crew of the *Rocinante.* It is
space opera, it is good, albeit American (way too many
firefights for my liking), space opera, and it is entertaining
and intriguing. The plot is rapid-paced -- this should be
something that even the puppies should enjoy... That said, I
understand that there are some serious problems in the physics
here and there (but as someone who forgets more than they
actually learned in secondary school physics, what I don't
notice doesn't burst my suspension of disbelief).

Where I have problems is with all the gun fights going on in
space stations and habitats and onboard ships. I am not an
engineer and I am not a physicist, but I do know that even with
the super-efficient Epstein fusion drive that mass is still
going to be an issue. I also know (or think that I know) that
you don't want to be shooting off automatic weapons and anti-
tank style weapons in a pressurised environment. So, you are
going to have to haul extra mass to make extra thick walls to
deal with the constant shootouts that take place out in the high
frontier. Of course, you could do something sensible and outlaw
this sort of weaponry. Would kind of fit with the "Belter code"

about placing everyone else at risk without their consent...
Anyway, that's my main quibble.

Oh, and the crew of the *Rocinante* should have had their luck run
out by now...

Cibola Burn
James S. A. Corey
Orbit   592 pgs
***

What I really liked about this series was that it was
interplanetary (rather than interstellar). At the end of
Abbadon's Gate, the context is changed and we can now have
interstellar settings. Didn't like this one as much as the
earlier novels; I assume it is setting things up for something
later in the series...

The Affinities
Robert Charles Wilson
Tor   304 pgs
*****

There is far more books on the market than it is possible to
read, even if one was unemployed and just did nothing but read
and fulfil their basic physical needs. This is in way an excuse
for my taking so long to discover Robert Charles Wilson as an
author. If I wasn't doing research for Hugo eligible works, I
would probably have remained oblivious of Wilson until the
Aurora voter's package came out.

Some reviewer gave this The Affinities a logline review:
"Divergent for to adult readers". Uh, no. While the two books
do possess the kernel idea that humankind can be sorted into a
finite number of personality trait-based communities and both
deal with issues of identity, this is all that they have in
common. Unlike Divergent, set in the typical YA future
dystopian society, The Affinities is set in contemporary
society, or just a couple of years in the future from now (then
2015). The Affinities are not social engineering or a method of
social control; they are about the new social phenomenon of
Affinity testing (involving genetic, neurological, and
psychological analysis that is then processed through some
proprietary algorithms) that qualifies you to enter into one of
twenty-two Affinity groups, or none at all. The novel's
protagonist, Adam Fisk, is sorted into the Tau Affinity. The

Tau Affinity becomes his new family; fellow members don't need to know you to understand you -- as they are also Tau -- everybody just gets everybody else. The Affinity groups are also those people whom with you can best co-operate with in all aspects of life.

The novel raises questions of identity, family, tribalism, our roles in society, and what is society, in manner that doesn't shy away from the complexity of these question and doesn't provide us with a neatly wrapped package of answers either. A fine, near future story.

However, what is really amazing is the author's deft skills as a writer. His descriptions, the dialogue, and the characters - the prose is simply excellent. I have since read Blind Lake and I have started the Spin trilogy (reviews to follow in the next issue) and I remain impressed by this author.

The Affinities is my pick for best novel published in 2015.

Flogging a Dead Trekkie: The SWILL Slates

Neil Jamieson-Williams

Why have a single slate, when you can have three? Lester is bemused by the slates, being ignorant of pretty much everything on them. Not to worry, Lester; I am certain that the average Puppy follower is in a similar position - they just nominate and vote as they have been told to.

So, we have a Hugo awards slate. Some of the categories are blank, because like Lester, I have no idea as to what I would nominate in the category. The categories with content (not unlike the Puppy slates) express a particular bias, in this case for speculative fiction content produced by my fellow citizens. I would really like to call attention to the SWILL suggestion for best fanzine, Auroran Lights; this is an excellent fanzine that, because it is also the official outlet of the organisation that organises the Aurora Awards (Canada's Hugos), can never be nominated or win in its own country. That said, readers should also strongly consider SWILL as their second choice for best fanzine - just because…

The Official SWILL Slate for the Hugo Awards

Best Novel:

The Affinities	Robert Charles Wilson
The Just City	Jo Walton
The Mechanical	Ian Tregillis
Aurora	Kim Stanely Robinson
The Heart Goes Last	Margaret Atwood
This Gulf of Time and Stars	Julie Czernada

Best Novella:

Best Novelette:

Best Short Story:

The Patent Bagger	Suzanne Church	AE The Canadian Science Fiction Review
La Héron	Charlotte Ashley	The Magazine of Fantasy & Science Fiction
The Practical Witch's Guide to Acquiring Real Estate	A.C. Wise	Uncanny Magazine
Two-Year Man	Kelly Robson	Asimov's Science Fiction
As Below, So Above	Matt Moore	Second Contacts (Bundoran Press)
Looking for Gordo	Robert J. Sawyer	Future Visions (Melcher Media)

Best Related Work:

Best Graphic Story:

Best Dramatic Presentation (Long Form):
The Martian
Predestination
Ex Machina
When Marnie Was There
Self/Less
Inside Out

Best Dramatic Presentation (Short Form):

The Man in the High Castle	Season 1
You, Me, and the Apocalypse	Series 1
The Expanse	Season 1 (episodes 1 - 4)
Orphan Black	Season 3
Continuum	Season 4
Haven	Season 5 (episodes 14 - 26)

Best Fanzine:
Auroran Lights
SWILL
Ecdysis
Opuntia
Broken Toys
WARP

Best Fancast:
Speculating, Canada (Trent Radio 92.7 FM) Derek Newman-Stille

Best Fan Writer:
Lester Rainsford (Ed Treijs)
R. Graeme Cameron
Dale Speirs
Taral Wayne
Jonathan Crowe
Neil Jamieson-Williams

Best Fan Artist:
Taral Wayne
Brad Foster
Zach Bellissimo
Steve Stiles
Jean-Pierre Normand
Keith Braithwaite

The next slate is for the FAAn Awards. These awards do not
permit you to nominate yourself or your zine - though I am
probably only bending the rules by recommending that you
nominate me and this wonderful zine…

The Official SWILL Slate for the FAAn Awards

Best Genzine:
Auroran Lights   R. Graeme Cameron
The Drink Tank   Chris Garcia
Ecdysis   Jonathan Crowe
Askance   John Purcell
Journey Planet   Garcia/Bacon
Interstellar Ramjet Scoop   Bill Wright

Best Perzine:
SWILL   Neil Jamieson-Williams
Vibrator   Graham Charnock
EAYOR   Chuck Conner
Opuntia   Dale Speirs
Counter Clock   Wolf von Witting
Broken Toys   Taral Wayne

Best Single Issue:

SWILL #28
Auroran Lights #17
Ecdysis #5
Journey Planet #21
EAYOR #3
Counter Clock #22

Best Fan Writer:
Lester Rainsford (Ed Treijs)
Mike Glyer
Chuck Conner
Dave Langford
Taral Wayne
Neil Jamieson-Williams

Best Fan Artist:
Brad Foster
Steve Stiles
D West
Zach Bellissimo
Jean-Pierre Normand
Taral Wayne

Best Letterhack:
Lloyd Penney
John Purcell
Robert Lichtman
Taral Wayne
Milt Stevens
Mike Meara

Best Fanzine Cover:
TightBeam #272   Jim Hatama
Counter Clock #23   Tais Teng
EAYOR #1   Zach Bellissimo
Auroran Lights #16   Jean-Pierre Normand
Askance #35   Steve Stiles
Auroran Lights #15   Taral Wayne

Best Fan Website:
eFanzines   Bill Burns
Ansible   Dave Langford
File 770   Mike Glyer
Canadian SF Fanzine Archive   R. Graeme Cameron
Fancyclopedia 3   Marc Olson
TangentOnline   Dave Truesdale

And now, for the one, truly important slate -

The Official SWILL Slate for the Aurora Awards

Best Novel:

The Affinities	Robert Charles Wilson
The Just City	Jo Walton
The Heart Goes Last	Margaret Atwood
This Gulf of Time and Stars	Julie E. Czerneda
Irona 700	Dave Duncan

Best YA Novel:

The Masked Truth	Kelley Armstrong
An Inheritance of Ashes	Leah Bobet
Storm	Amanda Sun
Type2	Alicia Hendley
The Midnight Games	David Neil Lee

Best Short Fiction:

The Patent Bagger	Suzanne Church	AE The Canadian SF Review
La Héron	Charlotte Ashley	The Magazine of Fantasy & Science Fiction
The Practical Witch's Guide to Acquiring Real Estate	A.C. Wise	Uncanny Magazine
Two-Year Man	Kelly Robson	Asimov's Science Fiction
As Below, So Above	Matt Moore	Second Contacts (Bundoran Press)
Looking for Gordo	Robert J. Sawyer	Future Visions (Melcher Media)

Best Graphic Novel:

We Stand On Guard	Brian K. Vaughan & Steve Skroce	Image Comics (#1 - #6)
Bait	Kris Sayer	Pulp Literature (Issue 5)
Bite	Kris Sayer	Pulp Literature (Issue 6)
The Tailor and the Dragon Archer	Mel Anastasiou	Pulp Literature (Issue 8)

Best Poem/Song:

From Alpha Centauri the Earth is a Blue Bowl of Fish Soup	Rhea Rose & Nicholas Kelly	Vancouver Symphony Orchestra
Elegy for WLC	David Clink	The Dalhousie Review
Auchindrain Inventory: Village Museum	Neile Graham	Interfictions
Morrigan's Song	Colleen Anderson	Heroic Fantasy Quarterly
At Stake	Evelyn Deshane	Eternal Haunted Summer

Best Related Work:

The Exile Book of New Canadian Noir	Claude Lalumiere & David Nickle (eds.)
Second Contacts	Michael Rimar & Hayden Trenholm (eds)
The Canadian Adventures of Jules Verne	John Robert Colombo & Jean-Louis Trudel
Pulp Literature	Mel Anastasiou & Jennifer Landels & Susan Pieters
Lackington's Magazine	Ranylt Richildis
Professor Challenger: New Worlds, Lost Places	J R Campbell & Charles Prepolec

Best Artist:

Dan J. O'Driscoll	Falcon's Egg, Second Contacts
JJ Lee	Pulp Literature (Issue 7 cover)
Albert Ball	Pulp Literature (Issue 8 cover)
Melissa Mary Duncan	Pulp Literature (Issue 5 cover)

Best Dramatic Presentation:

Continuum Season 4	Simon Barry	Reunion Pictures
Orphan Black Season 3	John Fawcett & Graeme Manson	Temple Street
Between Season 1	David Cormican	Elevation Pictures
God Is an Iron	Bruce J. Lambie	Black Box & Mainline Theatre
Saving Hope (eps 42-60)	Malcolm MacRury & Morwyn Brebner	ICF Films

Best Fan Publication:

SWILL	Neil Jamieson-Williams	Issues #26 - #29
Ecdysis	Jonathan Crowe	Issues #5 - #6
Opuntia	Dale Speirs	Issues #296 - #330
Broken Toys	Taral Wayne	Issues #35 - #45
WARP	Cathy Palmer-Lister	Issues #90 - #93

Best Fan Organisational:

Derek Künsken & Marie Bilodeau   Can-Con 2015: Oct 30-Nov 1
Alana Otis-Wood & Paul Roberts   Ad Astra 34: April 10 - 12
Randy McCharles   WWC 2015: August 14-16

Best Fan Music:

Everbody Hates Elves (album)   Kari Maaren

Best Fan Related Work:

Lester Rainsford   Pissing on a Pile of Old Amazings
                       SWILL (#26 - #29)
Steve Fahnestalk   Amazing Stories (columns), Jan. 2, 2015
                       - Dec. 18, 2015
R. Graeme Cameron   Amazing Stories (columns), Jan. 2, 2015
                       - Dec. 11, 2015

Scribbling on the Bog Wall
Letters of Comment

Neil Jamieson-Williams

As I write this, we are back to a single LoC. My comments are, of course, in glorious pudmonkey.

1706-24 Eva Rd.
Etobicoke, ON
M9C 2B2

December 23, 2015

Greetings, O Lords of SWILL!

And, thank you for issue 29. How are you droogy boys, anyway? I am getting a fast loc done just before the Big Day, and you guys are next.

Sorry I didn't get to see you at SFContario. our only plans for that weekend were to go to the con for Sunday. When we found out the length of the Auroras ceremony would be about the same as the programming track on Sunday, we figured, why buy a membership, even a Sunday membership? We wouldn't be able to see anything, we'd be in the Aurora brunch. So, we attended only that, a few people were unhappy with us for that, and we got the usual hotel
brunch, and a very nice ceremony, the last of the pointy Franklin Johnson design. We also discovered that we received very, VERY few votes past our nomination, so I think Auroras are a thing of the past for us.

Too bad we missed each other. Ah, you never know; you could still get Aurora nominations... See in this issue, the SWILL slate does recommend you.

My, my, Rebecca Longspear-Jones has issues. Even if she is a
pseudonym. With those remarks, she might be running herself to
be the Republican candidate for the US presidency. Hey, we're
all going to hell! At least we'll be warm. won't have to shovel
any driveways!

Well, she is the illegitimate child of good old Reverend B.J.
Jones and Alicia Longspear (both contributors in the original
SWILL days), so there is no doubt that she is a Republican
supporter. If the any of the fundamentalist versions of the
Abrahamic God are correct – I'll be going to hell. The good
news is that I will have lots of company. And if the Abrahamic
demi-god of evil (aka Satan) is not up to the task, then I'll just
have to get some souls of the damned together to storm heaven.

America is exceptional, in so many negative ways. I have been
amazed at how many friends on Facebook has expressed some
measure of envy at the election of Justin Trudeau as prime
minister. Many of those friends also know, sometimes first-hand,
at how poorly the rest of the world looks at them, and they try
their best to be better than what others think of them. I hope
the future is not American, or Canadian, or British, or Russian,
or Chinese. I
hope the future is human.

Well, we were embarrassed for almost a decade with our federal
government; it'll now be their turn. Unless, though I doubt that
the powers that be in the USA would allow it, Sanders wins the
Democratic leadership and the election…

I am the type who's going to stick with the SF I know and
remember well, especially seeing that it's affordable. Gerrold,
Dick, Niven, and more. Fortunately, I have a couple of shelves
of that, so my New Year's resolution is to get back to reading
and enjoying what I grew up with.

I do some of that, that's what my Scribd account is used for. But I also like to keep somewhat current. However, there is so much out there now – there is no way you can keep on top of it.

The locol. Chris Garcia is right, there's a portion of fanzine fandom who seem to judge if something if Trufannish or not. They probably don't realize that few care what they think, if we ever did, and there is a growing percentage of fanzine fans who may not know who these judges are, or even suspected their presence. Chris doesn't mention that like many zines, I receive them, and I write a letter of comment. I think the next issue of Journey Planet is their LoC issue, so I think I might have a few letters in there.

I continue to give the mild jab here and there to the "trufen", but I don't give a shit about what they have to say. If fanzines do continue to survive, and I hope that they do, these "judges" of fannishness have already lost their old gatekeeper roles.

Ah, just like fiction, there is just too much to read with fanzines these days. I read some, I almost never LoC; and I read a bunch around this time of year when it is awards season...

I think that has already happened to some degree
The genre of SF has spread out so much, to cover so many interests, and to many different interests in the realm of the general public, I can see the term supergenre. It is spreading out so thinly as to become part of everyday life for that general public. It is no longer a proud and lonely thing to be a fan; we've been absorbed in Borg-like fashion.

It is no longer a special status to be a fan, unless you are a tradfan. But, genfandom is now the majority. As I said many issues ago, we won (sort of) but it has resulted in (from a tradfannish perspective) a triumph of the "mundanes". Most people read some speculative fiction and many more watch speculative fiction in the non-print mediums, but few are tradfans and even fewer are trufen. It's change, but not necessarily a bad one. As I have also stated previously, we live a world that in many ways has become science fictional…

Our next convention where we will be selling our merchandise will be Ad Astra 2016, about four months from now. I am now selling some of our jewelry through Spencer's Mercantile in Hamilton, and I am keeping track of any craft shows that have been past, so I can contact them well ahead of time in 2016, and see if I can get a table there.

Anyway.the Merriest of Christmases and Happiest of New Years to both you Chief Inquisitors. Is Rebecca Longspear-Jones your boss here, or did she just come up with the idea? The best for both of you and your families, and all hail the SWILL Inquisition, which no one expected, Monty Python style.

Off this goes to the snitch line. See you next year!

Yours, Lloyd Penney.

Hope you had a great holiday season. Catch you at Ad Astra — there will be a SWILL party

Endnote: Annual SWILL Message

Neil Jamieson-Williams

Greetings SWILLites and other reprobates…

Well it's 2016. Another year.

We're off to a good start here at home. The Conservatives have
been voted out and we now have a Liberal government. So far, so
good. While most Canadians are optimistic about the change; I
am just cautiously optimistic. The federal Liberal party no
longer occupies the centre on the political spectrum, but the
centre-right (where the old Progressive-Conservative party used
to reside). That said, better a party of the centre-right than
the further right USA Republican wanna-be Conservative party.

South of the border -- who knows what is going to happen. We
should have a clearer picture once the March flurry of primaries
are over with. I'm not certain which is more mind-boggling,
President Trump or President Sanders...

In the world of speculative fiction, the Puppies are back. They
should release their slates soon and we'll see how the
nominations go. I suspect that they will not be able to game
the nominations as easily as they did last year.

SFContario 6 66/100 will be a relaxicon this year and a two day
event only. I know that Lester will be going, though I may not
make the trek in from glorious Dundas.

Art Wanted:
SWILL is looking for cover art (front and back). Black and
white or colour. It can be humourous. It can be in poor taste.
It can be silly and irreverent. It just needs to be SWILLish.
Infamy awaits. Please send your submissions to:
swill@uldunemedia.ca

Pith Helmet and Propeller Beanie Tour

April 29 - May1 2016 Ad Astra -- Richmond Hill
                      SWILL Party will be held

Bye Bye

Puppies

CODA

A list of SWILL volumes:

Original SWILL	issues 1 through 7
SWILL 2011	issues 8 through 12
SWILL 2012	issues 13 through 17
SWILL 2013	issues 18 through 22
SWILL 2014	issues 23 through 26
SWILL 2015	issues 27 through 30
SWILL 2016/2017	issues 31 through 35
SWILL Annuals: Volume 1	issues 36 through 40

Vile Fen Press

a division of Klatha Entertainment an Uldune Media company

www.ingramcontent.com/pod-product-compliance
Lightning Source LLC
Chambersburg PA
CBHW081256040426
42452CB00014B/2525